INTERNATIONAL CENTRE FOR MECHANICAL SCIENCES

COURSES AND LECTURES No. 175

TOPICS
IN
COMBINATORIAL OPTIMIZATION

EDITED BY
S. RINALDI
TECHNICAL UNIVERSITY
OF MILANO

SPRINGER - VERLAG   WIEN - NEW YORK

ISBN 978-3-211-81339-3   ISBN 978-3-7091-3291-3 (eBook)
DOI 10.1007/978-3-7091-3291-3

PREFACE

In recent years, the need for a review of the state of the art in Combinatorial Optimization has been felt by many scientists and researchers in the field. The opportunity of achieving this aim was offered by the Deputy Secretary General of the International Centre of Mechanical Sciences, Professor A. Marzollo, who invited the contributors of this volume to Udine for a Workshop. During the meeting the participants discussed their results and their ideas on the future developments of the various facets of this expanding area of applied mathematics. The success of the Workshop and the encouragement of the participants suggested that I collect the main contributions in the present volume. It is my hope that it may both give a sound background to people entering this fascinating area of study and stimulate further research in the field.

The Editor
Sergio Rinaldi

LIST OF CONTRIBUTORS

BARTHES, J.P.: Département d'informatique et de Mathématiques Appliquées – Université de Technologie de Compiègne – 60200 Compiègne, France.

LAWLER, E.L.: Dept. of Electrical Engineering and Computer Science – University of California at Berkeley – U.S.A.

LUCCIO, F.: Università di Pisa – Pisa – Italy.

MAFFIOLI, F.: Istituto di Elettrotecnica ed Elettronica and Centro di Telecomunicazioni Spaziali of C.N.R. – Politecnico di Milano – Milano – Italy.

MARTELLI, A.: Istituto di Elaborazione dell'Informazione del C.N.R. – Via S. Maria, 46 – Pisa – Italy.

MONTANARI, U: Istituto di Elaborazione dell'Informazione del C.N.R. – Via S. Maria, 46 – Pisa – Italy.

RINALDI, S.: Istituto di Elettrotecnica ed Elettronica – Politecnico di Milano – Milano – Italy.

CONTENTS

CONTENTS

COMPUTING SHORTEST PATHS IN NETWORKS (*)

E.L. Lawler (**)

1. Introduction

The finding of shortest paths in networks is one of the most basic combinatorial optimization problems, and the algorithms for solving these problems are among the most widely used. The reader is probably aware that a variety of optimization problems, some of which appear to have little to do with paths in networks, can be formulated as shortest path problems.

There is a very large literature on algorithms for solving shortest path problems. In this chapter, we review only three of the most basic such algorithms and discuss their computational complexity.

2. Bellman-Ford Algorithm

Let $G = (N, A)$ be a directed graph with node set N and arc set A. Let the length of arc (i,j) be a_{ij} . ($a_{ij} = + \infty$, if arc (i,j) does not exist). The arc lengths may be positive or negative, but we require that no directed cycle have negative length.

Suppose we wish to find a shortest path from node 1 (the "origin") to each of the other nodes, 2, 3, . . . , n. Let

u_i = the length of a shortest path from node 1 to node i.

Clearly $u_i = 0$. For the other nodes, it is easily verified that

$$u_i = \min_{k \neq i} \{u_k + a_{ki}\}$$

This gives us a set of n-1 nonlinear equations which can be solved by a method of successive approximations, as follows.

Let

$$u_1^{(0)} = 0$$

(*)   This work has been supported by the U.S. Air Force Office of Scientific Research Grant 71-2076.

(**) Dept. of Electrical Engineering and Computer Science, University of California at Berkeley, U.S.A.

$$u_i^{(0)} = + \infty, \qquad i \neq 1.$$

Then

(2.1)
$$u_i^{(m)} = \min \left\{ u_i^{(m-1)}, \min_{k \neq i} \left\{ u_k^{(m-1)} + a_{ki} \right\} \right\}$$

Clearly, for all i, $u_i^{(m)} \leqslant u_i^{(m-1)}$, and we assert that $u_i^{(n-1)} = u_i$, the desired shortest path length.

We justify the above assertion as follows. Let $u_i^{(m)}$ be given the following interpretation :

$u_i^{(m)}$ = the length of a shortest path from node 1 to node i,

subject to the constraint that the path contains no more than m arcs.

Then a shortest path from 1 to i which contains no more than m arcs actually contains no more than m-1 arcs and is therefore $u_i^{(m-1)}$ in length, or else it contains an initial segment of m-1 arcs to some node k, of length $u_k^{(m-1)}$, and a final arc (k, i), of length a_{ki}. The equations (2.1) thus fit the interpretation of $u_i^{(m)}$ given above.

Finally, we note that because of the absence of negative directed cycles these can be no shortest path with more than n-1 arcs. Hence $u_i^{(m-1)} = u_i$, as claimed.

We must solve equations (2.1) for m = 1, 2, . . . ,n-1 and for i = 2, 3, . . . ,n. The solution of each equation requires n-1 additions and n-1 comparisons. Hence, the overall computation requires on the order of n^3 additions and n^3 comparisons.

J.Yen has proposed improvements in the computation which reduce the number of additions and comparisons by a factor of approximately 4. However, even, with this improvement, the overall computational complexity is still $0(n^3)$, and this remains the most favorable complexity that has been attained for this problem. In the next section, we show that if all arc lengths are positive, an $0(n^2)$ computation is possible.

Admittedly, the algorithm we have described computes only the lengths of shortest paths and not the shortest paths themselves. By maintaining a record of the values of k for which the minimum is attained in the equations (2.1), the actual shortest paths can easily be constructed.

A similar version of this algorithm can also be employed to find shortest paths between all pairs of nodes in the network. However, this yields an $0(n^3 \log n)$ computation which is inferior to Floyd's method, described in section 4 below.

3. Dijkstra's Mehtod

Now suppose all arc lengths a_{ij} are positive. A method due to Dijkstra yields an $0(n^2)$ computation.

We begin by assigning the "label" $u_1 = 0$ to the origin and $u_i = +\infty$ to each of the other nodes. At each stage some of these labels are designated as "permanent" and others as "tentative". Initially only u_1 is permanent. The general step of the procedure is as follows. Find the tentatively labeled node k for which u_k is minimal (if there is a tie, break it arbitrarily). Declare node k to be permanently labeled, and revise the remaining tentative labels u_i by comparing u_i with $u_k + a_{ki}$ and replacing u_i by the smaller of the two values. The procedure terminates when all nodes are permanently labeled.

The proof of the validity of the method is inductive. At each stage the nodes are partitioned into two sets P (permanently labeled) and T (tentatively labeled). Assume the label of each node in P is the length of a shortest path from the origin, whereas the label of each node i in T is the length of a shortest path, subject to the constraint that each node in the path (except i) belongs to P. Then the node k in T with the smallest label can be transferred to P, because of a shorter path from the origin existed, it would have to contain a first node in T. However, such a node would have to be further away from the origin than k, since its label is larger than that of node k. The subsequent use of node k to reduce the labels of adjacent nodes belonging to T restores to T the property assumed above.

An analysis of the algorithm shows that, for a complete network, $n(n - 1)/2$ additions and $(n - 1)(n - 2)$ comparisons are required. Thus, the algorithm is $0(n^2)$ in complexity.

4. Floyd-Warshall Method

A computational method due to Floyd and to Warshall finds shortest paths between all pairs of nodes in $0(n^3)$ steps.

Define $u_{ij}^{(m)}$ as follows. Let

$u_{ij}^{(m)}$ = the length of a shortest path from i to j, subject to the condition that the path does not pass through nodes m, m + 1, . . . ,n (i and j excepted).

A shortest path from node i to node j which does not pass through nodes m + 1, m + 2, . . . ,n either (a) does not pass through node m, in which case $u_{ij}^{(m+1)} = u_{ij}^{(m)}$ or else (b) does pass through node m, in which case

$$u_{ij}^{(m+1)} = u_{im}^{(m)} + u_{mj}^{(m)} .$$

Thus we have

(4.1)
$$u_{ij}^{(1)} = a_{ij}$$

$$u_{ij}^{(m+1)} = \min \left\{ u_{ij}^{(m)} , u_{im}^{(m)} + u_{mj}^{(m)} \right\}$$

Clearly, $u_{ij}^{(n+1)} = u_{ij}$, the length of a shortest path from i to j.

We note that $u_{ij}^{(m)} = 0$, for all i and all m. It follows that there are exactly $n^3 - 3n^2$ equations (4.1) which require explicit solution, each by a single addition and a single comparison. Thus the method requires exactly $n^3 - 3n^2$ additions and the same number of comparisons.

REFERENCES

[1]   R.E. Bellman, "On a Routing Problem", Quart. Appl. Math., 16, (April 1958) 87-90.

[2]   E.W. Dijkstra, "A Note on Two Problems in Connexion with Graphs", Numerische Mathematik, 1 (1959) 269-271.

[3]   R.W. Floyd, "Algorithm 97, Shortest Path", Comm. ACM, 5 (June 1962) 345.

[4]   E.L. Lawler, "Shortest Paths", Chapter 3 of Combinatorial Optimization, to be published by Holt, Rinehart and Winston.

[5]   S. Warshall, "A Theorem on Boolean Matrices", J. ACM, 9 (1962), 11-12.

OPTIMAL UNCONSTRAINED CYCLES IN GRAPHS(*)

S.Rinaldi(**)

1. INTRODUCTION

This chapter is devoted to the problem of finding optimal cycles in graphs.

Let $G = (N,A)$ be a finite and oriented graph with $N = \{1,2,\ldots,n\}$ and a cost $c_{ij} \geqq 0$ associated with every arc $(i,j) \in A$.
The graph G is supposed to be strongly connected : this property implies the existence of at least one closed path (cycle) passing through any node of the graph.

In many applications, particularly in those related with transportation problems where the nodes of the graph represent cities, ports, or airports, the time required to accomplish a transition from i to j does depend upon the pair (i,j) so that a second weight $t_{ij} > 0$, called "transit time", is associated with every arc of the graph.

The problem of finding the optimal unconstrained cycle in G can be given the following formulation.

Problem 1.1. A finite, oriented, strongly connected, linear graph $G = (N,A)$ is given and a cost $c_{ij} \geqq 0$ and a time $t_{ij} > 0$ are associated to each arc $(i,j) \in A$. Let

$$\tau(\gamma) = \sum_{\gamma} t_{ij}$$

$$\mathcal{C}(\gamma) = \sum_{\gamma} c_{ij}$$

be the "length" and the "cost" of any cycle γ in the graph and let E be the set of all elementary cycles.

(*) This work has been supported by Centro Teoria dei Sistemi, Milano, Italy

(**) Istituto di Elettrotecnica ed Elettronica del Politecnico di Milano, Italy.

Then, determine the cycle $\gamma^0 \in E$ with minimum average cost, i.e.

$$c^0 = C(\gamma^0) = \min_{\gamma \in E} C(\gamma) = \min_{\gamma \in E} \frac{\mathcal{C}(\gamma)}{\tau(\gamma)} = \min_{\gamma \in E} \frac{\sum_\gamma c_{ij}}{\sum_\gamma t_{ij}} \ .$$

In the next section the equivalence between this problem (from now on called Periodic Optimization problem) and the one dealt with in the preceding chapter in the asymptotic case is shown (see Romanowskii [1], Treiger and Gill [2] and Rinaldi [3]). This entails that Problem 1.1. can be considered as the deterministic version of the well known problem of asymptotic optimization of finite Markov chains (see Howard [4] and [5]). The policy iteration procedure for Markov chains optimization (see Howard [5]) is then briefly described in Section 3 and it is shown how this procedure fails in the deterministic case. Therefore, this computation scheme is slightly modified (following Fillières [6]) in order to obtain a convergent algorithm. Then, Problem 1.1. is formulated in terms of Linear Programming in Section 4 and an algorithm, quite similar to the preceding one, is derived by looking at the dual problem (see Romonowskii [1] and Dantzig et al.[7]). A third algorithm, due to Lawler [8], and based on the search of negative cycles in a graph is described in Section 5. The advantage of this algorithm is that it requires (in the worst possible case) less computational effort than either of the two preceding algorithms or the obvious dynamic programming procedure which is presented, for completeness, in Section 6. Finally, some of the applications which motivated the study of the problem are discussed in Section 7.

2. PRELIMINARY REMARKS

A first important remark relative to the properties of the optimal cycle γ^0 consists of noticing that the paths π obtained by decomposition of the cycle γ^0 are not, in general, optimal paths.

To prove this one can consider the graph with all transit times t_{ij} equal to one and with the costs c_{ij} given as in Fig. 2.1. (no entry in the cost matrix means no arc). The cycle $(1, 2, 3, 7, 1)$ is an optimal cycle γ^0, but the path $\pi = (1, 2, 3)$, which is a part of γ^0, is in no sense an optimal path from node 1 to node 3. In fact, both the paths from 1 to 3 with minimum total cost and with minimum average cost are constituted by the arc $(1, 3)$.

Therefore, one can not expect the problem of Periodic optimization to be strictly related with the problem of optimal paths in graphs. Nevertheless, a relation between these two problems actually exists (see Theorem 2.1). Now, consider the case with unity transit times and let $\mathcal{C}_i(t)$ be the cost of a least-costly path starting from node i and containing t arcs and let $C_i(t) = \mathcal{C}_i(t)/t$ be the cost-to-time ratio of such a path. Obviously, if the graph G is strongly connected the dependence of $C_i(t)$ upon node i vanishes for t going to infinity. In other words, there exists a constant K such that

$$\lim_{t \to \infty} C_i(t) = K \qquad \forall i . \tag{2.1}$$

This result, which is not even proved here, is due to Bellman [9], while a short and elegant proof can be found in Romanowskii [1].

The constant K in eq. (2.1) is the minimum cost to time ratio of all infinite paths in the graph G (asymptotic optimization problem).

An important result proved by Romanowskii [1] and then by Traiger and Gill [2], (certainly considered as known by many other authors as Kaufman and Cruon [10] and Fillières [6]) consists in noticing that the problem of asymptotic optimization is equivalent to Problem 1.1 in the sense that $K = C^0$. Hence, the problem of the determination of the cycle γ^0 with average cost C^0 turns out to be related with the problem of finding optimal paths in graphs (functions $\mathcal{C}_i(t)$).

Recalling that the classical problem of optimization of Markov chains (see Howard [4] and [5]) is the extension to the probabilistic case of the asymptotic optimization problem considered above, one can conclude that Problem 1.1. is simply the deterministic version of the problem of optimization of Markov chains over an infinite horizon of time. Then, all the methods known for the solution of such a problem (see, for example, Howard [5] and Rinaldi and Rozzoni [11] are candidates for the solution of the problem, and actually, in the next section an algorithm is derived by slightly modifying the well known Howard's policy iteration procedure. The equivalence of the problems of asymptotic and periodic optimization is now proved by means of a result (Lemma 2.1.) which is of interest from a computational point of view.

Lemma 2.1.

If

$$\underline{C}(t) = \min_i C_i(t) \qquad \overline{C}(t) = \max_i C_i(t)$$

then
(2.2) $\underline{C}(t) \leqslant C^0 \leqslant \bar{C}(t)$

where C^0 is the minimum average cost of all cycles in the graph.

Proof

The proof is in two parts: (i) $\underline{C}(t) \leqslant C^0$ and (ii) $C^0 \leqslant \bar{C}(t)$.

(i)   Let N^0 be the set of nodes of γ^0 and let k be its cardinality.
Consider the path starting from node $i \in N^0$ and containing exactly t
arcs of γ^0 and let $\ell_i^*(t)$ be its total cost. Obviously,

$$\ell_i(t) \leqslant \ell_i^*(t) \qquad \forall i \in N^0$$

But

$$\sum_{i \in N^0} \ell_i^*(t) = kC^0 t$$

and, therefore,

$$\sum_{i \in N^0} C_i(t) \leqslant kC^0 .$$

This implies $C_i(t) \leqslant C^0$ for at least one $i \in N^0$. Since, by definition,
$\underline{C}(t) \leqslant C_i(t)$ the first inequality of eq. (2.2) follows.

(ii)   Consider the paths with minimum total cost starting from every
node and containing exactly t arcs. The path starting from node
$n_0 \triangleq 1$ terminates in node n_1, the path starting from n_1 terminates in
node n_2 and so on. Let ℓ be the first integer such that $n_\ell = n_{\ell - h}$
for some $h \leqslant \ell$. Thus, let $\bar{\gamma}$ be the cycle (in general this cycle is not
elementary) containing the path from $n_{\ell - h}$ to $n_{\ell - h + 1}$ followed by
the path from $n_{\ell - h + 1}$ to $n_{\ell - h + 2}$ and so on up to $n_\ell = n_{\ell - h}$.
Since, in general, $\bar{\gamma}$ is not a solution of the Periodic Optimization
problem, one has $C(\bar{\gamma}) \geqslant C^0$.

But

$$C(\bar{\gamma}) = \frac{\ell(\bar{\gamma})}{\tau(\bar{\gamma})} = \frac{\sum_{i = n_{\ell - h}}^{n_{\ell} - 1} \ell_i(t)}{ht} ,$$

hence

$$\sum_{i=n_{\ell-h}}^{n_{\ell-1}} C_i(t) \geqslant hc^0 \; .$$

Thus, $C_i(t) \geqslant C^0$ for at least one node i from which the second inequality of eq. (2.2) follows. $\square$

Eq. (2.1) and Lemma 2.1. imply the following result of equivalence.

Theorem 2.1.

Given a finite and strongly connected linear graph $G = (N,A)$ with costs $c_{ij} \geqslant 0$ and transit time $t_{ij} > 0$ associated to each arc $(i, j) \in A$, the minimum average cost C^0 of all elementary cycles is equal to the minimum cost-to-time ratio K of all infinite paths.

The assumption of the graph being strongly connected can actually be removed in Theorem 2.1 and substituted by a weaker assumption (existence of a cycle in the graph). On the contrary, the assumption of the graph being finite is essential as one can easily check by means of a counter-example.

3. A DETERMINISTIC VERSION OF THE POLICY ITERATION PROCEDURE FOR MARKOV CHAINS OPTIMIZATION

Theorem 2.1. of the preceding section says that Problem 1.1. is equivalent to the problem of asymptotic optimization of finite Markov chains in the deterministic case.

As it is well known, a finite Markov chain is a stochastic system described by an n x n transition matrix $P_{ij} = [p_{ij}]$, where p_{ij} is the probability of transition $i \to j$; in other words, if the system is in state $i \in X$ at time t, then there is a probability p_{ij} that the system is in state $j \in X$ at time $t + 1$. Thus, $0 \leqslant p_{ij} \leqslant 1$ and $\sum_{j=1}^{n} p_{ij} = 1$. A cost $c_{ij} \geqslant 0$ and a transit time $t_{ij} > 0$ are associated to $i \to j$, and, in general, either the probabilities p_{ij} and the costs and transit times c_{ij} and t_{ij} depend upon an input variable, here called "decision". Now, suppose we observe the state of the system before any transition and, on the basis of this observation we select a decision. Thus, let d_i be the decision associated with state i and write

$$p_{ij} = p_{ij}(d_i) \qquad c_{ij} = c_{ij}(d_i) \qquad t_{ij} = t_{ij}(d_i) \; .$$

The dynamic behavior of the system is known (of course in a probabilistic sense) if a control law $X \to U$ is given, namely if a decision d_i is associated to every state i of the system (following the tradition any control law $d = (d_1\, d_2\, ,\dots, d_n\,)$ is here called a "policy"). In fact, given a policy d it is possible to compute the probabilities $p_i(t)$ of being in state i at time t. In general, this probability $p_i(t)$ depends upon the initial state and an important class of Markov chains (called "completely ergodic" in the following) is characterized by the property that for any policy d the limit $p_i(d)$ of $p_i(.)$ for t going to infinity exists and is independent of the initial conditions. If a Markov chain is completely ergodic one can associate to every policy d the expected value of a cost-to-time ratio C(d). In fact, let

$$\mathcal{C}_i\,(d) = \sum_{j=1}^{n} p_{ij}\,(d_i\,)c_{ij}\,(d_i\,)$$

$$t_i\,(d) = \sum_{j=1}^{n} p_{ij}\,(d_i\,)t_{ij}\,(d_i\,)$$

and denote by $\mathcal{C}\,(d)$ and $t(d)$ the expected value of the cost and transit time of a transition when the system is in "asymptotic conditions". Thus,

$$\mathcal{C}(d) = \sum_{i=1}^{n} p_i\,(d)\mathcal{C}_i\,(d)$$

$$t(d) = \sum_{i=1}^{n} p_i\,(d)\,t_i\,(d)$$

and the ratio

(3.1)
$$C(d) = \frac{\mathcal{C}(d)}{t(d)}$$

represents the expected value of the cost-to-time ratio in the asymptotic behavior. If C(d) is determined by means of eq. (3.1), the asymptotic probabilities $p_i(d)$ must be first calculated. Nevertheless, C(d) can be more easily determined (for a proof see Howard [5]) by solving the following linear equations

(3.2)
$$v_i + Ct_i = \mathcal{C}_i + \sum_{j=1}^{n} p_{ij}\, v_j \qquad\qquad i = 1,\dots,n.$$

This system of n equations in n + 1 unknowns (C and v_i) always has an infinity of solutions if the system is completely ergodic. This infinity of solutions is characterized by a unique value of C and by unique relative values of the v_i's, from now on called "potentials" (this property can be easily checked recalling that $\sum_{j=1}^{n} {}^{\cdot}|p_{ij} = 1)$. Eq. (3.2) gives

$$C = \frac{\mathcal{C}_i}{t_i} + \frac{\sum_{j=1}^{n} p_{ij} \; v_j - v_i}{t_i} \qquad i = 1, ..., n \qquad (3.3)$$

which states that the cost-to-time ratio C is the sum of the cost rate $\mathcal{C}_i/t_i$ for each state and a quantity which can be considered as the contribution to C derived from state i's relation to the other states of the system.

The problem of asymptotic optimization of Markov chains is to find that policy d^0 with the minimum average cost C^0, namely

$$C^0 = C(d^0) = \min_{d} C(d) . \qquad (3.4)$$

Eqs. (3.2) and (3.3) are the basis for solving problem (3.4) by means of the well known policy iteration procedure (see Howard [5]). Such an iterative procedure operates in two steps: evaluation of the potentials and evaluation of the policy. In the first step the potentials v_i^t and the cost C_t associated to the t-th iteration are computed by means of eq. (3.2) once the policy d^t is known. In the second step the new policy d^{t+1} is obtained by minimizing for each i the right hand side of eq. (3.3) with $v_i = v_i^t$, i.e., by solving the equations

$$\min_{d_i} \left[\frac{\sum_{j=1}^{n} p_{ij} \; (d_i) c_{ij} \; (d_i)}{\sum_{j=1}^{n} p_{ij} \; (d_i) t_{ij} \; (d_i)} + \frac{\sum_{j=1}^{n} p_{ij} \; (d_i) v_j^t - v_i^t}{\sum_{j=1}^{n} p_{ij} \; (d_i) t_{ij} \; (d_i)} \right] \qquad i = 1, ..., n.$$

Given an initial policy, the method converges to the optimal solution in a finite number of iterations (a proof of this fact can be found in Howard [5]).

Now, let us consider the deterministic version of the problem. For any given j, the probabilities $p_{ij} \; (d_i)$ are all zero but one which is unity, so that a particular transition $i \rightarrow j$ is associated to the decision d_i. In other words, in the deterministic case, a policy is more simply a function $j(.): X \rightarrow X$ given by $i \rightarrow j(i)$.

The first important remark is that a deterministic Markov chain is not, in general, completely ergodic, since, given an initial state and a policy $j(.)$, the state where the system will be after t transitions is uniquely identified. In other words, for any state i the probabilities $p_i(t)$ are either null or unity and, apart from particular cases, $p_i(.)$ does not have a limit for $t \to \infty$. If, for example, the system is the one considered in Section 2 (see Fig. 2.1) and the policy is

$$(3.5) \qquad j(.) = (j(1), j(2), \dots, j(7)) = (2,3,7,7,3,5,1)$$

as shown in Fig. 3.1.a, then $p_i(t) = 0$ for $i = 4,5,6$ and $t > 1$ while the functions $p_i(.)$ $i = 1,2,3,7$ are periodic ($p_i(t) = p_i(t + 4)$)) and do not have a limit for $t \to \infty$. If, on the converse, the policy is

$$(3.6) \qquad j(.) = (3,3,4,3,3,7,7)$$

as represented in Fig. 3.1.b, the functions $p_i(.)$ have a limit for some initial conditions (for example if $x(0) = 6$ or $x(0) = 7$) while for some others not.

Nevertheless, though the system is not completely ergodic, it is possible to particularize the iterative procedure described above to the deterministic case. In order to do this, let $j_t(.)$ be the policy of the t-th iteration, and, if the system is described by means of a graph $G = (N, A)$, let associate to each policy $j_t(.)$ the graph $G_t = (N, A_t)$, $A_t = \{(i, j_t(i)), i \in N\}$, which, for obvious reasons, is called the "representation" of $j_t(.)$ (the two graphs of Fig. 3.1. are, for example, the representations of the policies (3.5) and (3.6)).

The graph G_t is, in general, constituted by a finite number of disconnected subgraphs G_t^k, $k = 1, \dots, m_t$, called components, and every component G_t^k contains one and only one cycle γ_t^k. In the following, a policy $j_t(.)$ is called "simple" when its representation contains only one component (i.e., when G_t is connected) and "multiple" in all other cases (for example, (3.5) is simple, while (3.6) is multiple).

Now, if the policy iteration procedure is particularized to the deterministic case, the following algorithm is obtained.

1.   Let $j_0(.)$ be a policy.
2.   Let $t = 0$.
3.   Put $v_1^t = 0$ and determine the "potentials" v_i^t, $i = 2,3, \dots, n$ and the average cost C_t by means of the equations

$$(3.7) \qquad v_i^t = v_{j_t(i)}^t + c_{ij_t(i)} - C_t \, t_{ij_t(i)} \; .$$

4.   Determine the new policy j_{t+1} (.) by solving for $i = 1,2, \ldots ,n$

(3.8) $\min_{j} \left[\dfrac{c_{ij}}{t_{ij}} + \dfrac{v_j^t - v_i^t}{t_{ij}} \right]$.

5.   If j_{t+1} (.) $= j_t(.)$ stop: the optimal cycle γ^0 is the cycle associated
        to the policy j_t (.).
        If j_{t+1} (.) $\neq J_t(.)$, increase t and go to 3.   □

It is important to note that eq. (3.7) with $v_1^t = 0$ cannot be solved for all $j_t(.)$. In
fact, C_t must be equal to the average cost $C_t^k = \sum_{\gamma_t^k} c_{ij} / \sum_{\gamma_t^k} t_{ij}$ of any cycle
γ_t^k associated to j_t (.). Hence, $j_t(.)$ must be either a simple policy or a multiple one
with all associated cycles γ_t^k with the same average cost ($C_t^k = C_t$ for all k). Such
policies will be called "regular" from now on. Thus, at least $j_0(.)$ must be regular.
Unfortunately this is not sufficient to get the convergence of the algorithm since eq.
(3.8) can generate a policy j_{t+1} (.) which is not regular, as the following example
shows.

Example 3.1.
        Let the costs c_{ij} be given as in Fig. 2.1 and let t_{ij} = 1 for all (i, j) $\in$ A.
        If the initial policy $j_0(.)$ is as in Fig. 3.2a (best cycle of lengthh 1), step
3 of the algorithm gives

$$(v_1^0 , v_2^0 , \ldots , v_n^0) = (0,-2,-8,-8,0,-6,-5) .$$

Thus, step 4 gives the new policy $j_1(.)$ represented in Fig. 3.2b. Since
$c_{77} \neq (c_{34} + c_{43})/2$ this policy is not regular and the next step of the algorithm, i.e.,
the solution of eq. (3.7) for t = 1 cannot be accomplished.   □

        In conclusion, the policy iteration procedure does not work, in general,
in the deterministic case since step 3 of the algorithm cannot always be
accomplished. Nevertheless, it can be proven that the algorithm converges when eq.
(3.8) generates only regular policies.

        Thus, an obvious and interesting way of modifying the algorithm is to
proceed as follows. Let j_{t_1} (.) be the first non-simple policy (of multiplicity m_{t_1})
given by eq. (3.8) and let $G_{t_1}^k$, k = 1, \ldots ,m_{t_1} be the components of j_{t_1} (.).
Moreover, let G_i , i = 1, \ldots .,m_{t_1} be the subgraph of G which has the nodes of
$G_{t_1}^i$ as set of nodes. Eq. (3.7) can be solved for every G_i separately and the
algorithm can be applied to every one of the subgraphs until eq. (3.8) gives a

non-simple policy for one of them. Of course the argument can be repeated (augmenting the number of the subgraphs) and the conclusion is that the algorithm converges in a finite number of iterations to a certain number of cycles which are the optimal ones in the subgraphs G_1.

Example 3.2.

We now apply the method just described to the example of Fig. 2.1.

Since the policy $j_1(.)$ is not simple (see Fig. 3.2.b), consider the two subgraphs G_1 and G_2 associated with the two components of this policy ($N_1 = (1, 2, 3, 4, 5)$ and $N_2 = (6, 7)$). The subgraphs G_1 and G_2 are described by the two submatrices of the costs c_{ij} indicated in Fig. 2.1. The policy iteration procedure applied to G_2 gives the selfloop $(7,7)$ (the subgraph G_2 coincides with the second component G_1^2 of $j_1(.)$), while the same procedure applied to G_1 gives the sequence of policies represented in Fig. 3.3. Nevertheless, the cycle $(4, 5, 4)$ which is optimal in the subgraph G_1, is not the optimal one in G as it is shown below.   □

Actually, one can do better than find suboptimal solutions by slightly modifying the policy iteration procedure just described. In fact, the following algorithm (an extension of the algorithm presented by Fillières [6] and of some optimality conditions given by Dorato [12]) will be proved to converge in a finite number of iterations to the optimal solution.

Algorithm 3.1.

1.   Let $j_0^*(.)$ be a policy

2.   Let $t = 0$.

3.   Determine the components G_t^{*k} associated to the policy $j_t^*(.)$ and the average costs C_t^{*k} of every cycle γ_t^{*k}.

4.   If $j_t^*(.)$ is regular put $j_t(.) = j_t^*(.)$ and go to 5.

           If $j_t^*(.)$ is not regular let γ_t be a cycle with minimum average cost among the cycles γ_t^{*k} and let C_t be its average cost. Then, construct a regular simple policy $j_t(.)$ which has γ_t as associated cycle and go to 5.

5.   For every cycle associated to $j_t(.)$ choose one node i* and put $v_{i*}^t = v_{i*}^{t-1}$ (for $t = 0$ put $v_1^t = 0$). Then, determine the potentials v_i^t for all other nodes by means of eqs. (3.7) which are rewritten here

$$(3.7) \qquad v_i^t = v_{j_t(i)}^t + c_{ij_t(i)} - C_t t_{ij_t(i)} \ .$$

6.   Determine the new policy j_{t+1}^* (.) by solving for all i eq. (3.8) which is

$$\min_{j} \left[\frac{c_{ij}}{t_{ij}} + \frac{v_j^t - v_i^t}{t_{ij}} \right] . \qquad (3.8)$$

If for a given node i there is indifference among some nodes j, let j_{t+1}^* (i) = j_t(i) if j_t(i) is one of these nodes, otherwise choose by means of the lexicographic rule.

7.   If j_{t+1}^* (.) = j_t^* (.) stop: all cycles associated to j_t^*(.) are optimal.

If j_{t+1}^* (.) ≠ j_t^*(.) increase t and go to 3.   □

Before proving the convergence of the algorithm let us apply it to the example described in Fig. 2.1. in order to have some insight into the method.

Example 3.3.

The first step of the algorithm is summarized in Fig. 3.2. which shows that the policiy j_1^* (.) has two components associated with it. The cycles associated with these two components are γ_1^{*1} = (3, 4, 3) and γ_1^{*2} = (7, 7). Since $C_1^{*1} < C_1^{*2}$ the policy j_1^* (.) is not regular. Hence step 4 of the algorithm gives, for example, the regular policy j_1(.) represented in Fig. 3.4. (to construct a regular policy one can substitute one arc (h, k) of every cycle $\gamma_t^{*k} \neq \gamma_t$ by an arc (h, ℓ) where ℓ is a node of γ_t : in our case (7, 7) has been substituted by (7, 3)). Thus, putting $v_3^1 = v_3^0$ and noticing that C_1 = 9/2, by means of eq. (3.7) one obtains

$$v^1 = \left(-\frac{13}{2} , -\frac{13}{2}, -3, -\frac{7}{2}, -\frac{11}{2}, \frac{3}{2}, 1 \right)$$

which allows to solve eq. (3.8) with t = 1. The result, i.e., the policy j_2^*(.) and all the following policies and potentials are shown in Fig. 3.4.

Since j_5^*(.) = j_6^*(.), the optimal cycle is the cycle (1, 2, 3, 7, 1) and C^0 = 9/4 (any potential is attached to its node).   □

Two main facts can be observed on the example. First the function C_t is not increasing ($C_{t+1} \leq C_t$) and, second, if $C_t = C_{t+1}$ ($C_2 = C_3$ in the example) then the potentials are not increasing ($v_i^{t+1} \leq v_i^t$). These two properties can be proved to hold in general.

Theorem 3.1.

For every t the following inequality holds

$$C_{t+1} \leqslant C_t .$$

Proof

Since

$$\min_j \left[\frac{c_{ij}}{t_{ij}} + \frac{v_j^t - v_i^t}{t_{ij}} \right] = \min \left\{ \frac{c_{ij_t(i)}}{t_{ij_t(i)}} + \frac{v_{j_t(i)}^t - v_i^t}{t_{ij_t(i)}} \; ; \min_{j \neq j_t(i)} \left[\frac{c_{ij}}{t_{ij}} + \frac{v_j^t - v_i^t}{t_{ij}} \right] \right\}$$

and (see eq. (3.7))

$$\frac{c_{ij_t(i)}}{t_{ij_t(i)}} + \frac{v_{j_t(i)}^t - v_i^t}{t_{ij_t(i)}} = C_t$$

eq. (3.8) implies

(3.9) $$c_{ij_{t+1}^*(i)} + v_{j_{t+1}^*(i)}^t - v_i^t \leqslant C_t \, t_{ij_{t+1}^*(i)} \qquad \forall \; i,t.$$

Thus, adding eq. (3.9) for all nodes i of any cycle γ_{t+1}^{*k} one obtains

$$C_{t+1}^{*k} \leqslant C_t .$$

Since $C_{t+1} = \min_k C_{t+1}^{*k}$ the theorem follows   □

Theorem 3.2.

If $C_{t+1} = C_t$ and $j_{t+1}(\cdot) \neq j_t(\cdot)$, then $v_i^{t+1} \leqslant v_i^t$ for all i and the strict inequality holds for at least one node i.

Proof

The fact $C_{t+1} = C_t$ implies that the policy is regular, i.e., $j_{t+1}^*(\cdot) = j_{t+1}(\cdot)$. Thus, from eq. (3.7) and $C_{t+1} = C_t$, it follows that

$$v_i^{t+1} = v_{j_{t+1}(i)}^{t+1} + c_{ij_{t+1}(i)} - C_t \, t_{ij_{t+1}(i)}$$

which, because of eq. (3.9), gives

(3.10) $$v_i^{t+1} \leqslant v_i^t + v_{j_{t+1}(i)}^{t+1} - v_{j_{t+1}(i)}^t \qquad \forall i.$$

Furthermore, since $j_{t+1}(.) \neq j_t(.)$ the strict inequality holds in eq. (3.10) for at least one node i.

Now consider the components G_{t+1}^k and call I^k the set of the nodes of the cycle γ_{t+1}^k. Moreover, let i^k be the node of I^k for which $v_{i^k}^{t+1} = v_{i^k}^t$ (see step 5 of the algorithm). Thus, for the nodes i which are predecessors of i^k (i.e., $j_{t+1}(i) = i^k$) eq. (3.10) gives

$$v_i^{t+1} \leqslant v_i^t \qquad \forall i : j_{t+1}(i) = i^k \qquad \text{for some k.} \qquad (2.3.11)$$

Now, let i be the nodes which are the predecessors of the nodes for which eq. (3.11) holds. For these nodes eqs. (3.10) and (3.11) still give

$$v_i^{t+1} \leqslant v_i^t .$$

Continuing this way until all nodes of the graph have been considered proves the theorem.   □

On the basis of these two theorems the convergence of the algorithm can now be proven.

Proof of Convergence

We must prove that

(a)   The algorithm converges (i.e., $j_{t+1}^*(.) = j_t^*(.)$ for a finite t).

(b)   The algorithm converges to the optimum $(j_{t+1}^*(.) = j_t^*(.)$ implies $C_t = C^0$ and $\gamma_t = \gamma^0$).

Proof of (a)

The number of policies is finite; therefore, there must exist a t and a $K \geqslant 1$ such that $j_t^*(.) = j_{t+K}^*(.)$. But, since C_t is not increasing, it must be $C_t = C_{t+1} = \ldots = C_{t+K}$ .Hence, from Theorem 3.2 it follows that $v_i^{t+h} \geqslant v_i^{t+h+1}$, i = 1, ... ,n, h = 0, 1, . . . ,K-1, and for every h there exists at least one i such that $v_i^{t+h} > v_i^{t+h+1}$. Since $v_i^t = v_i^{t+h}$, it follows that K = 1.

Proof of (b)

Suppose $j_{t+1}^*(.) = j_t^*(.)$.
From eq. (3.8) it follows that

$$\frac{c_{ij^*_{t+1}}(i)}{t_{ij^*_{t+1}}(i)} - \frac{v_{j^*_{t+1}}(i) - v_i^t}{t_{ij^*_{t+1}}(i)} \leqslant \frac{c_{ij}}{t_{ij}} + \frac{v_j^t - v_i^t}{t_{ij}} \ .$$

Thus, eq. (3.7) and $j^*_{t+1}(i) = j^*_t(i)$ give

$$C_t \, t_{ij} \leqslant c_{ij} + v_j^t - v_i^t \qquad \forall i,j .$$

Hence, for every cycle γ in the graph

$$\frac{\sum_\gamma c_{ij}}{\sum_\gamma t_{ij}} \geqslant C_t \ . \qquad \qquad \square$$

Something can be said about the computational complexity of Algorithm 3.1. In fact, suppose all data (c_{ij} , t_{ij}) are integer numbers and $|c_{ij}| \leqslant \alpha$ and $t_{ij} \leqslant \tau$. Since every cycle γ is constituted by at most n arcs we have $\sum_\gamma t_{ij} \leqslant n\tau$; therefore, if γ_1 and γ_2 are two cycles with different average cost, then

$$\left| \frac{\sum_{\gamma_1} c_{ij}}{\sum_{\gamma_1} t_{ij}} - \frac{\sum_{\gamma_2} c_{ij}}{\sum_{\gamma_2} t_{ij}} \right| \geqslant \frac{1}{n^2 \tau^2} \ .$$

Thus, every time that $C_{t+1} < C_t$ in the preceding algorithm, one knows that

$$C_{t+1} \leqslant C_t - \frac{1}{n^2 \tau^2} \ ,$$

which implies that the number of iterations characterized by $C_{t+1} \neq C_t$ is bounded by $2\alpha n^2 \tau^2$ (since, obviously, $-\alpha \leqslant c^0 \leqslant \alpha$,). But, the complexity of any iteration is $O(n^2)$ additions and comparisons (see eq. (3.8)); hence the complexity of the algorithm is at least $O(n^4)$ (at least since the iterations with $C_{t+1} = C_t$ have not been taken into account). Thus, from this point of view this algorithm is worse than the one of Lawler (see Section 5) which is $O(n^3 \log n)$ in complexity. Nevertheless, in all the numerical examples which have been handled, the procedure presented here turned out to be better than that of Lawler, since the number of iterations required to reach the optimum was incomparably less than $2^{\alpha n^2 \tau^2}$ (for instance, in the example considered above, $2\alpha \bar{n}^2 \tau^2 = 980$ while the number of iterations required by the algorithm is 6).

4. LINEAR PROGRAMMING SOLUTION

The purpose of this section is to show how Problem 1.1. can be formulated as a Linear Programming problem and how an algorithm, similar to the one presented in the preceding section, can be devised from this formulation. This way of approaching the problem is essentially due to Dantzig et al. [7] and Romanowskii [1] who independently proposed the same algorithm for solving the problem.

Consider the following non-linear integer programming problem

$$\min_{x_{ij}} \frac{\sum_{i,j} c_{ij} x_{ij}}{\sum_{i,j} t_{ij} x_{ij}} \qquad (4.1a)$$

subject to

$$\sum_i x_{ij} = \sum_k x_{jk} \qquad j = 1,\dots,n \qquad (4.1b)$$

$$x_{ij} = \text{non-negative integer.} \qquad (4.1c)$$

A configuration in the graph $G = (N, A)$ is obviously associated to every feasible solution of this problem. The variable x_{ij} represents the number of times the arc (i, j) is in the configuration and eq. (4.1b) implies that this configuration is actually the union of elementary cycles. In particular, a feasible solution of problem (4.1) can always be associated to any elementary cycle γ. But more than this can be said, since any elementary cycle γ^0 which is an optimal solution of Problem 1.1 is an optimal solution of problem (4.1). In fact, a feasible solution of problem (4.1) constitued by a set of cycles γ cannot be optimal if one of these cycles has an average cost $\sum_\gamma c_{ij} / \sum_\gamma t_{ij}$ lower than some of the others. Therefore, the optimal solution of problem (4.1) is either associated to an elementary cycle γ^0 or the union of cycles γ^0 (some of which are eventually repeated).

Now, let us associate to problem (4.1) the following Linear Programming problem

(4.2a)
$$\min_{y_{ij}} \ \sum_{i,j} c_{ij} \ y_{ij}$$

subject to

(4.2b)
$$\sum_i y_{ij} = \sum_k y_{jk} \qquad j = 1, \dots, n$$

(4.2c)
$$\sum_{i,j} t_{ij} \ y_{ij} = 1$$

(4.2d)
$$y_{ij} \geq 0$$

and suppose (only in order to have a more simple and homogeneous discussion) that the costs c_{ij} and the transit times t_{ij} are integer numbers. Thus, any optimal solution y_{ij}^0 of problem (4.2) can be given the form

(4.3)
$$y_{ij}^0 = \frac{z_{ij}^0}{\tau}$$

where z_{ij}^0 is a non-negative integer and τ is a positive integer.

From eqs. (4.2b) and (4.3) it follows that

$$\sum_i z_{ij}^0 = \sum_k z_{jk}^0 \qquad j = 1, \dots, n$$

which implies z_{ij}^0 is a feasible solution of problem (4.1). Actually, it can be proved that z_{ij}^0 is an optimal solution of problem (4.1). To show this, note first that problem (4.2) with the two extra-contraints

(4.4a)
$$y_{ij} = \frac{z_{ij}}{\sum_{i,j} t_{ij} \ z_{ij}}$$

(4.4b)
$$z_{ij} = \text{non-negative integer}$$

is equivalent to problem (4.1). But y_{ij}^0 and z_{ij}^0 satisfying eq. (4.3) satisfy also eqs. (4.4) since from (4.2c) it follows

$$\sum_{i,j} t_{ij} \ z_{ij}^0 = \tau .$$

Therefore, (y_{ij}^0, z_{ij}^0) is an optimal solution of problem (4.2, 4.4).

In conclusion, an optimal solution γ^0 of Problem 2.1. can be obtained by solving the Linear Programming problem (4.2) and by putting the solution y_{ij}^0 of such a problem in the form (4.3). The integers z_{ij}^0 allow us to detect a cycle γ^0 or the union of some optimal cycles γ^0. The procedure which gives a cycle γ^0 from the integers z_{ij}^0 is not even described since it is obvious and can, anyway, be derived by an analogous procedure presented in the next chapter for a more complex problem (see Section 6).

Of course, the Linear Programming problem (4.2) can be solved by means of the "simplex" method or by any other method such as the "out of kilter" method (in this case the computational effort at any iteration is greater, but the convergence is obtained in a lower number of iterations, (see Fox [13]). Nevertheless, this approach presents a few inconveniencies. First of all, it requires that a general Linear Programming algorithm is available to the operator and, second, some extra-analysis is needed to obtain the optimal cycle γ^0. Fortunately, a more direct algorithm can be obtained by forcing the optimal solution of the Linear Programming problem to be an elementary cycle.

This algorithm can be induced either by slightly modifying the "simplex" method (see (Dantzig et al. [7]) or, equivalent, by referring to the dual of problem (4.2) (see Romanowskii [1]). This second equivalently way of looking at the problem is the one we follow.

Thus, consider the general Linear Programming problem

$$\min_{u} \quad c'u \tag{4.5a}$$

subject to

$$Au = b \tag{4.5b}$$

$$u \geqslant 0 \tag{4.5c}$$

where b is an r-dimensional vector, c and u are s-dimensional vectors ((c' is the row vector obtained from c by transposition) and A is an r x s matrix and recall (see Dantzig [14]) that the "dual" of such a problem is, by definition,

$$\max_{v} \quad b'v \tag{4.6a}$$

subject to

$$A'v \leqslant c \tag{4.6b}$$

and that u^0 and v^0 are the optimal solutions of the two problems if and only if

(4.7) $[A'v^0]_i = c_i$ $\forall i : u_i^0 > 0$

where $[A'v^0]_i$ and c_i stay for the i-th components of the vectors $A'v^0$ and c, respectively.

In our case, problem (4.5) is the Linear Programming problem (4.2), so that $r = n + 1$, $s = n^2$ and

$$u' = \left(y_{11}\ y_{12}\ \cdots\ y_{1n} \ \vdots\ y_{21}\ y_{22}\ \cdots\ y_{2n}\ \vdots\ \cdots \right)$$

$$c' = \left(c_{11}\ c_{12}\ \cdots\ c_{1n} \ \vdots\ c_{21}\ c_{22}\ \cdots\ c_{2n}\ \vdots\ \cdots \right)$$

$$b' = \left(0\ \ 0\ \ \cdots\ 0\ \ 1 \right)$$

$$
A = \begin{bmatrix}
0 & 1 & 1 & \cdots & 1 & \vdots & -1 & 0 & 0 & \cdots & 0 & \vdots \\
0 & -1 & 0 & \cdots & 0 & \vdots & 1 & 0 & 1 & \cdots & 1 & \vdots \\
0 & 0 & -1 & \cdots & 0 & \vdots & 0 & 0 & -1 & \cdots & 0 & \vdots \\
\vdots & \vdots & \vdots & & \vdots & \vdots & \vdots & \vdots & \vdots & & \vdots & \vdots & \cdots \\
0 & 0 & 0 & \cdots & -1 & \vdots & 0 & 0 & 0 & \cdots & -1 & \vdots \\
t_{11} & t_{12} & t_{13} & \cdots & t_{1n} & \vdots & t_{21} & t_{22} & t_{23} & \cdots & t_{2n} & \vdots
\end{bmatrix}
$$

Therefore, if v_i, $i = 1, \ldots, n$ is the i-th component of the vector v and C is its (n + 1)-st component the dual problem (4.6) becomes

(4.8a) $\max_{v} C$

such that

(4.8b) $v_i - v_j + Ct_{ij} \leq c_{ij}$.

Moreover, if (C^0, v_i^0) is the optimal solution of such a problem, from eq. (4.7) it follows that

(4.9) $v_i^0 - v_j^0 + C^0 t_{ij} = c_{ij}$

for all pairs (i, j) such that $y_{ij}^0 > 0$. Since at least one optimal solution of problem (4.2) is associated to an elementary cycle, our problem can be solved by looking for a cycle γ^0 a set of potentials v_i^0 and an average cost C^0 such that

$$v_i^0 - v_j^0 + C^0 t_{ij} = c_{ij} \qquad \text{if } (i,j) \text{ belongs to } \gamma^0 \qquad (4.10a)$$

$$v_i^0 - v_j^0 + C^0 t_{ij} \leqslant c_{ij} \qquad \text{otherwise.} \qquad (4.10b)$$

Obviously, C^0 is the average cost of γ^0 (see eq. (4.10a)).

The actual determination of (γ^0, v_i^0, C^0) can be carried out by means of the following algorithm.

Algorithm 4.1.
1.　　　　Let $J_0(.)$ be a simple policy.
2.　　　　Let $t = 0$.
3.　　　　Determine the cycle γ_t associated to the policy $j_t(.)$ and let C_t be its average value.
4.　　　　Put $v_i(t) = 0$ for a node i of the cycle γ_t. Then, compute all the other potentials $v_i(t)$ by means of the equation

$$v_i^t = v_{j_t(i)}^t + c_{ij_t(i)} - C_t t_{ij_t(i)} . \qquad (4.11)$$

5.　　　　Check if the inequality

$$v_i^t \leqslant v_j^t + c_{ij} - C_t t_{ij} \qquad (4.12)$$

is satisfied for all the arcs (i, j) which do not belong to the cycle γ_t. If this is the case, then γ_t is an optimal cycle. If for an arc (i, j) eq. (4.12) is not satisfied let $j_{t+1}^*(.)$ be the policy obtained by substituting in the representation G_t of $j_t(.)$ the arc $(i, j_t(i))$ by the arc (i, j).

6.　　　　If $j_{t+1}^*(.)$ is a simple policy put $j_{t+1}(.) = j_{t+1}^*(.)$, increase t and go to 3. If $j_{t+1}^*(.)$ is not a simple policy it contains in its representation G_{t+1}^* a cycle γ^* and the cycle γ_t. Thus, replace one of the arcs of γ_t, say arc (h, k), by an arc (h, ℓ) where ℓ is any node of γ_{t+1}^*, so obtaining a new simple policy $j_{t+1}(.)$. Finally, increase t and go to 3. □

When improving the policy from $j_t(.)$ to $j_{t+1}(.)$ (see steps 5 and 6 of the algorithm) two cases are possible: (1) node j does not precede node i in the graph G_t which represents the policy $j_t(.)$ (i.e., there is no path from j to i in G_t); (2) node j precedes node i. In the first case $\gamma_{t+1} = \gamma_t$ and only the potentials of the predecessors of j in G_{t+1} are different from the potentials of the t-th iteration. In case (2) $\gamma_{t+1} \neq \gamma_t$, $C_{t+1} < C_t$ and all the potentials must be recalculated.

On the basis of these simple remarks it is possible to prove that Algorithm 4.1 converges in a finite number of iterations to the optimal solution (C^0, γ^0) and that every iteration is characterized by $C_{t+1} \leqslant C_t$. The proof of these properties is not given here since it is quite similar to that of the preceding section.

The Algorithm presented in this section turns out to be very similar to Algorithm 3.1. The potentials v_i^t are, in fact, determined by means of the same equation, so that the two algorithms differ only in the evaluation of the policy j_{t+1} (.) from the potentials v_i^t. If Algorithm 3.1 is used the policy j_{t+1} (.) can be completely different from the policy j_t(.), while if Algorithm 4.1 is used the representations G_t and G_{t+1} of the policies j_t(.) and j_{t+1} (.) can differ at most for two arcs. Therefore, Algorithm 4.1 is, in some sense, more "conservative" than Algorithm 3.1.

Example 4.1.

The same example we have been dealing with in the preceding sections (see Fig. 2.1.) is now reconsidered.

Let the initial j_0 (.) be as in Fig. 4.1a, where the corresponding potentials (determined by means of eq. (4.11)) are also shown (each one attached to its node) and, execute step 5 of Algorithm 4.1 by following the lexicographic ordering (11, 12, . . . , 1n; 21, 22, . . . , 2n; . . .). Since the first arc (i, j) for which inequality (4.12) is not satisfied turns out to be arc (1, 2), it follows that arc (1.7) must be replaced by arc (1, 2). Thus, the simple policy j_1(.) represented in Fig. 4.1b is obtained and the potentials v_i^1 are all unchanged but v_1^1, which is determined by means of eq. (4.11).

Now inequality (4.12) is checked again and the first arc for which this equation is not satisfied is arc (1,3). Therefore, the simple policy j_2(.) represented in 4.1c is obtained and the new potentials v_i^2 can be computed again. Continuing this way the policy j_5 (.) turns out to be the one shown in Fig. 4.2a. The first arc (i,j) not satisfying eq. (4.12) is now the arc (3, 4) so that the non-simple policy j_6^*(.) represented in Fig. 4.2b is obtained by replacing arc (3,7) by arc (3,4). We now execute step 6 of the algorithm by replacing the selfloop (7,7) by the arc (7,3) and we get the simple policy j_6(.) shown in Fig. 4.2c.

Then, one can continue until the optimal solution is obtained.   □

A few remarks are suggested by Example 4.1. First of all one should note that Algorithm 3.1 is considerably more sophisticated than Algorithm 4.1 in the policy evaluation, since this operation is accomplished by means of a minimization over all the nodes of the graph while the present method is more "local", the policy being changed as soon as the first possible improvement is revealed by the non satisfaction of eq. (4.12). Therefore, the number of iterations required by the method presented in this section to reach the optimum shoud be considerably greater than the one required by Algorithm 3.1 and this is indeed in good agreement with the experience the author has on the problem.

Nevertheless, it is fair to notice that if Algorithm 4.1 is well organized, the fact that more iterations are required does not entail a much higher computational complexity. In fact, the number of elementary operations required to accomplish one iteration by means of Algorithm 4.1 is often very small when $\gamma_{t+1} = \gamma_t$, since, in this case, only a subset of the potentials must be computed (those associated with the predecessors of node j in G_{t+1}).

5. A BINARY SEARCH PROCEDURE

A third method (see Lawler [8]) for solving the Periodic Optimization problem is now presented.

Given a graph $G = (N,A)$ with weights $\bar{c}_{ij}$ associated to each arc $(i,j) \epsilon A$, the sign of a cycle γ with respect to (w.r.t.) the weights $\bar{c}_{ij}$ is defined as the sign of $\sum_{\gamma} \bar{c}_{ij}$. Moreover, suppose one knows an algorithm for detecting a negative cycle (if any) in a finite graph (for a recent review on this subject see Yen [15]).

Now, let C be a guessed value for the minimum average cost C^0 and associate a new cost

$$\bar{c}_{ij} (C) = c_{ij} - Ct_{ij}$$

to each arc $(i,j) \epsilon A$.

Then, one of the following three situations must arise.

Case 1.   There is an elementary cycle γ which is negative w.r.t. $\bar{c}_{ij}$ (C).

Case 2.   All elementary cycles are positive w.r.t. $\bar{c}_{ij}$ (C).

Case 3.   All elementary cycles are non-negative w.r.t. $\bar{c}_{ij}$ (C) and at least one of them is a zero-cost cycle.

If case 1 holds and γ is a negative cycle w.r.t. $\bar{c}_{ij}$ (C), then

$$\sum_{\gamma} \bar{c}_{ij} \; (C) = \sum_{\gamma} c_{ij} - C \sum_{\gamma} t_{ij} < 0.$$

Since $t_{ij} > 0 \; \forall (i,j) \in A$, it follows that

$$C^0 \leqslant C(\gamma) = \sum_{\gamma} c_{ij} \, / \sum_{\gamma} t_{ij} < C,$$

namely, the guessed value C is too large and γ is a cycle the average cost of which is strictly smaller than C.

For the same reasons, $C < C^0$ in Case 2 and $C = C^0$ in Case 3.

These properties suggest two different search procedures based on the testing of the existence of negative cycles in G w.r.t. $\bar{c}_{ij}$ (C) for successive values of C: "monotonic" and "binary" search.

A monotonic search consits in choosing an initial value C_1 greater than or equal to the minimum average cost C^0 and then, test for the existence of negative cycles in G w.r.t. $\bar{c}_{ij}$ (C_1). If Case 1 holds (as is usually the case) a negative cycle γ_2 is obtained and its average cost is $C_2 < C_1$. Thus, the procedure is iterated and a sequence of values

$$C_1 > C_2 > C_3 > \ldots$$

is obtained until some C_s is found for which Case 3 holds ($C_s = C^0$). Now, remember (see Section 3) that if $|c_{ij}| \leqslant \alpha$ and $t_{ij} \leqslant \tau$, two elementary cycles γ_1 and γ_2 with different average costs $C(\gamma_1)$ and $C(\gamma_2)$ are such that

$$|C(\gamma_1) - C(\gamma_2)| \geqslant \frac{1}{n^2 \tau^2}.$$

Thus, taking $C_1 = \alpha$, from the inequalities $-\alpha \leqslant C^0 \leqslant \alpha$ it follows that

(5.1) $s \leqslant 2\alpha\tau^2 n^2 .$

On the other hand, a binary search can be devised as follows. Suppose we know an interval of uncertainty (a,b) for C^0. We first try the value $C_1 = (a + b)/2$. If Case 1 holds we know that C^0 is contained in the interval $(a,(a + b)/2)$. If Case 2 holds the optimum average cost is in the interval $((a + b)/2,b)$, while if Case 3 holds we have $C^0 = C_1$. We continue in this way, halving the remaining interval at each iteration so that after k times the length of the interval of uncertainty cannot be greater than $(b-a)2^{-k}$. The interval-halving procedure ends when Case 3 holds or when

$$\frac{b-a}{2^s} \leqslant \frac{1}{n^2\tau^2},$$

(5.2)

since, after that, only one distinct average cost (namely the optimal one) can lie within the interval of uncertainty (actually this cost can be found by testing for negative cycles w.r.t. $\bar{c}_{ij}$ (b)). Thus, from eq. (5.2) with b-a = 2^α it follows that the number of steps required by the binary search to reach the optimum in the worst possible case is

$$s \leqslant 1 + \log_2\alpha + 2\log_2\tau + 2\log_2 n.$$

(5.3)

A comparison between the bounds (5.1) and (5.3) is in favor of the binary search, since $\log_2 n \ll n^2$ for large values of n. In conclusion, the binary search procedure can be summarized as follows.

Algorithm 5.1

1.   Let $a \leqslant C^0 \leqslant b$ (for example a = $- \alpha$, b = α).
2.   If b-a $\leqslant 1/(n^2\tau^2)$ let C = b. Otherwise, let C = (a +b)/2 be an estimate of C^0.
3.   Evaluate $\bar{c}_{ij}$ (C) = $c_{ij} - Ct_{ij}$.
4.   Test for negative cycles w.r.t. $\bar{c}_{ij}$ (C) .
5.   If Case 1 holds let b = C and go to 2.
                 If Case 2 holds let a = C and go to 2.
                 If Case 3 holds C^0 = C. Stop.   □

The problem of finding a negative cycle (if any) in a graph G with costs $\bar{c}_{ij}$ (see point 4 of Algorithm 5.1) can be solved by adaptation of well known shortest path algorithms which, in general, require $O(n^3)$ computational steps, where n is the number of nodes of G. One of the most effective algorithms of this type (see Yen [16]) is now described and the adaptation to the problem of detecting a negative cycle in a graph is pointed out.

The algorithm works for graphs with no selfloops, but this is in no sense a restriction, since given a graph G = (N,A) with costs $\bar{c}_{ij}$ one can first test for the existence of a negative $\bar{c}_{ii}$,and then, if such a $\bar{c}_{ii}$ does not exist, disregard all selfloops, since a negative elementary cycle (if any) will not contain any slefloop.

Thus, suppose there is no selfloop in the graph and call an arc (i,j) "rightward" if i< j and "leftward" if i >j. A path is said to contain a change in direction whenever a rightward arc is followed by a leftward arc, or vice versa. Now, let

$\bar{c}_i (m) \overset{\Delta}{=}$ the cost of a least-costly path from node 1 to node i such that the path contains no more than m changes in direction.

In particular, for m = 0, we have

$$\bar{c}_1(0) = \infty$$

since there is no path from 1 to 1 with an even number of changes in direction (in general $\bar{c}_1(m) = \bar{c}_1(m-1)$ if m is even). Moreover,

$$\bar{c}_2(0) = \bar{c}_{12}$$

$$\bar{c}_3(0) = \min [\bar{c}_{13} ; (\bar{c}_{12} + \bar{c}_{23})]$$

$$\bar{c}_4(0) = \min [\bar{c}_{14} ; \min_{1 \leqslant k < 4} (\bar{c}_k(0) + \bar{c}_{k4})]$$

and, in general,

$$(5.4) \qquad \bar{c}_i(0) = \min [\bar{c}_{1i} ; \min_{1 \leqslant k < i} (\bar{c}_k(0) + \bar{c}_{ki})] \qquad i = 2,3,\dots,n.$$

Now, let us increase m from the value 0 to the value 1, i.e., let us consider the paths which contain at most one change in direction.
Obviously,

$$\bar{c}_n(1) = \bar{c}_n(0) ,$$

since there is no path from 1 to n with an odd number of changes in direction (in general $\bar{c}_n(m) = \bar{c}_n(m-1)$ if m is odd). Moreover,

$$\bar{c}_i(1) = \min [\bar{c}_i(0); \min_{i < k \leqslant n} (\bar{c}_k(1) + \bar{c}_{ki})] \qquad i = n-1, n-2, \dots, 1.$$

By induction, one obtains the following iterative procedure for computing the costs $\bar{c}_i(m)$ from the costs $\bar{c}_i(m-1)$.

Iterative procedure

1.   Let $\bar{c}_i(0)$ be given as in (5.4).

2.   If m is even let

$$\bar{c}_1(m) = \bar{c}_1(m-1)$$

and then solve for i = 2, 3, . . . , n the equation

$$\bar{c}_i(m) = \min\,[\,\bar{c}_i(m-1)\,;\,\min_{i<k\leqslant n}\,(\bar{c}_k(m)+\bar{c}_{ki}\,)\,].\qquad\qquad (5.5)$$

3.   If m is odd let

$$\bar{c}_n(m) = \bar{c}_n(m-1)$$

and then solve for i = n-1, n-2, . . . ,1 the equation

$$\bar{c}_i(m) = \min\,[\,\bar{c}_i(m-1)\,;\,\min_{1\leqslant k<i}\,(\bar{c}_k(m)+\bar{c}_{ki}\,)\,].\qquad\qquad (5.6)$$
$$\square$$

If $c_1(m) < 0$ for some $m > 0$ the procedure can be stopped since there exists a negative cycle in the graph (actually there exists a negative cycle passing through node 1). On the converse, if $c_i(m+2) = c_i(m)$ for all i and for some $m > 0$, obviously, there are no negative cycles in the graph. Now, observe that a shortest path from node 1 to every node of the graph exists if and only if there is no negative cycle in the graph. On the other hand, a shortest path (if any) from node 1 to node i does not contain more than n-2 changes in direction. Hence the following necessary and sufficient condition for the existence of negative cycles w.r.t. $\bar{c}_{ij}$ holds.

Theorem 5.1.

A graph G contains a negative cycle w.r.t. the costs $\bar{c}_{ij}$ if and only if $\bar{c}_i(n-1) < \bar{c}_i(n-2)$ for at least one i = 1, . . . ,n in the iterative procedure above. $\square$

It follows that in the worst possible case eqs. (5.5) and (5.6) must be solved for m = 1, . . . , n-1.

Since each equation is solved by a minimization over about n/2 alternatives, on the average, the number of additions and comparisons required is approximately $1/2\,n^3$.

In conclusion, if we are concerned with the population of problems with similar cost and time parameter values, in the sense that α and τ are invariant with n, then the number of negative cycles computations is simply proportional to $\log_2 n$ (see eq. (5.3)) and the overall computation is $O(n^3\log_2 n)$. Hence, the number of elementary operations is bounded by a polynomial function in the number of states of the system, which means that the problem of Periodic Optimization can be considered to be a well-solved combinatorial optimization problem.

6. DYNAMIC PROGRAMMING APPROACH

Problem 1.1. can, of course, be solved by means of Dynamic Programming (see, for instance, Lawler [8] and Shapiro [17]).

Although the problem can be solved in general, for the sake of simplicity in notation only the particular case where the transit times t_{ij}, are all equal to one is considered in this section.

Thus, given a graph $G = (N,A)$ with costs $c_{ij} \gtrless 0$ and times $t_{ij} = 1$, let $f_{ij}(m) \triangleq$ the cost of a least-costly path from node i to node j containing exactly m arcs.

Obviously,

$$(6.1) \qquad f_{ij}(1) = c_{ij} \qquad (f_{ij} = \infty \text{ if } (i,j) \notin A)$$

and

$$(6.2) \qquad f_{ij}(m) = \min_{k} (c_{ik} + f_{kj}(m-1)) \qquad m = 2,3,\ldots,n.$$

Hence, the Periodic Optimization Problem can be solved by means of the equation

$$(6.3) \qquad \min_{i,m} \frac{f_{ii}(m)}{m}.$$

Since in eq. (6.2) i, j and m assume the values $1,2,\ldots,n$ and the minimization is carried over n alternatives it follows that the complexity of the computation is $O(n^4)$ additions and comparisons. Thus, despite the fact that we are in the particular case $t_{ij} = 1$, dynamic programming approach seems to be always worse than the binary search method for large scale systems. The only advantage of this method is that it is definitely the most simple to program.

The traditional way of solving eqs. (6.2) is to compute the matrix $[f_{ij}(m)]$ from the matrix $[f_{ij}(m-1)]$. Operating in this way one must record such matrices for $m = 1,\ldots,n$ in order to be able to detect the optimal cycle γ^0 after solving eq. (6.3). Hence, a total of n matrices of dimension n x n must be stored, i.e., the memory space is $O(n^3)$.

Nevertheless, there is a different way of solving the problem which requires storing only one matrix of dimension n x n. Hence, this method (proposed by Aris et al. [18] in a different context and called the "cut state" method) is n times better than the traditional method from the point of view of the storage requirement.

The cut state method proceeds as follows. Let j = 1 and solve eq. (6.2) for all values of i and m. For each pair (i,m) a node k is obtained which minimizes the right-hand-side of eq. (6.2). Therefore, an n x n matrix K can be filled, every entry (i,m) of which is represented by such a node k. When eq. (6.2) has been solved for j = 1 and for all values of i and m, one can solve the problem

$$\min_m \frac{f_{11}(m)}{m}$$

and hence determine the optimal cycle passing through node 1 by simply analyzing the matrix K.

Then, the procedure can be repeated for j = 2 and so forth using the same memory space given by the matrix K at every iteration. After the last iteration has been accomplished, the best cycle among n cycles must be found.

In conclusion, the complexity of this procedure is still $O(n^4)$ additions and comparisons, but it is only $O(n^2)$ in memory space.

An interesting property of the cut state method is that it is the one requiring the minimum memory space among all possible iterative procedures for solving the problem (for a proof of this see Bertelè and Brioschi [19]).

7. EXAMPLES

Three examples, chosen among those which have been presented in the literature, are described in this section. Other examples of application such as PERT-cost schemes, optimal serving systems and industrial scheduling can be found in Romanowskii [1] and Cunningham-Green [20].

(a) A scheduling problem

Let us consider the following scheduling problem (see Kaufmann and Cruon [10]). A machine is operated in time and can, at the beginning of each period (year), either be replaced or maintained in service. Suppose that any equipment which is n years old is subject to obligatory replacement. Thus, if x(t) indicates the age of the equipment at the beginning of the t-th year just before the possible replacement one has x(t + 1) = x(t) + 1 if the machinery is maintained in service and x(t + 1) = r(t) + 1 if the equipment is replaced by one of age r(t). Hence, the system has n states ($x(t) = 1, \ldots, n$) and can be described on a complete graph with transit times $t_{ij} = 1$ and costs c_{ij} associated to each arc. The transition from node i to node j can be interpreted as the following sequence of operations: (1) sell equipment of age i, (2) buy equipment of age (j-1), (3) maintain in service this equipment for one year (of course, the operations (1) and (2) do not make sense when i = j-1). Therefore, a profit p_i (the value of a machinery of age i) is associated to operation (1), while a cost c_j (purchase and maintenance costs) is associated to operations (2) and (3). In conclusion the transition from i to j has a cost c_{ij} associated with it given by

(7.1)
$$c_{ij} = c_j - p_i .$$

and the problem of determining the optimal periodic schedule is

$$\min_{\gamma \in E} \frac{\sum_\gamma c_{ij}}{\sum_\gamma t_{ij}} .$$

The structure of the data, i.e., the particular form of the costs c_{ij} given by eq. (7.1), implies that the optimal solution is the optimal selfloop. In fact, if N_γ is the set of nodes of any cycle γ, from eq. (7.1), it follows that

$$\sum_\gamma c_{ij} = \sum_{i \in N_\gamma} (c_i - p_i) .$$

Therefore, the average cost $C(\gamma)$ of any cycle is a convex combination of the average costs of the selfloops associated to the nodes of the cycle, and this entails that the best cycle is the selfloop with minimum average cost $c_i - p_i$.

Of course, if there are additional costs in the system, eq. (7.1) is not satisfied any more. Thus, the optimal schedule is not so trivial and one of the algorithms described above must be used to solve the problem. This is, for example, the case when one considers the well known problem "When should I change my car?". In this case, in fact, an extra tax must be payed every time the car is replaced, and this can justify a different policy than using every year a car of the same age.

(b)   **Optimal parallel computations**

Many models for parallel computations which have appeared in the literature represent the calculation as a directed graph in which nodes and arcs are, respectively, processing units and data channels. One of such models is here described (for more details see Reiter [21]) and it is shown how the optimal schedule of a parallel computation can be found by solving a Periodic Optimization problem. Let $G = (N,A)$ be a finite graph where $N = \{1, \ldots, n\}$ represent the set of "operators" and $A = \{(i,j)\}$ the set of "data channels". The initial number of data words on channel (i,j) is d_{ij}, while t_{ij}, is the time required for operator i to place the result of its operation on branch (i,j) (in other words, if operator i initiates at time t, then at time $t + t_{ij}$ one data word is placed on channel (i,j)).

For example, suppose one must solve the following system of difference equations

$$x_{i+1} = y_i z_i - x_i$$

$$y_{i+1} = |x_i + y_i| + x_i z_i$$

$$z_{i+1} = x_i y_i / z_i$$

with x_0, y_0 and z_0 given. Then a possible computation graph is given in Fig. 7.1, where the initial data (zero or one word) are shown on the arcs. Every node represents one of the following elementary operations: addition ($+$), subtraction ($-$), absolute value $|\cdot|$, multiplication ($\times$) and division ($./.$). If one unit of time is required by the first two operations, 2 units by absolute value, 3 by multiplication and 4 by division, one obtains the matrices $[d_{ij}]$ and $[t_{ij}]$ of Fig. 7.2 (no entry means no arc).

Now, let σ_i^k be the time of the k-th initiation of operator i so that the matrix

$$S = \begin{vmatrix} \sigma_1^1 & \sigma_1^2 & \sigma_1^3 \ldots \\ \sigma_2^1 & \sigma_2^2 & \sigma_2^3 \ldots \\ \vdots & \vdots & \vdots \\ \sigma_n^1 & \sigma_n^2 & \sigma_n^3 \ldots \end{vmatrix}$$

represents a schedule. In order to be feasible, a schedule S must be such that at least one data word is on channel (i,j) when operator j is initiated or, to say it in a different way, if $b_{ij}(t)$ denotes the number of data words or arc (i,j) at time t it must be

$$b_{ij}(\sigma_j^k) \geqslant 1 \qquad \forall k, \; \forall (i,j) \in A . \tag{7.2}$$

For obvious reasons, a particular but important class of schedules is the one of periodic schedules P_T given by

$$P_T = \begin{vmatrix} t_1 & t_1 + T & t_1 + 2T\dots \\ t_2 & t_2 + T & t_2 + 2T\dots \\ \vdots & \vdots & \vdots \\ t_n & t_n + T & t_n + 2T\dots \end{vmatrix}$$

Thus, an interesting problem is to find the periodic schedule with minimum period T, since this entails the highest rate of computation. In other words, the following problem must be solved

$$(7.3) \qquad T_m = \min_{P_T} (T | P_T \text{ is feasible}) .$$

We now show how this problem can be reduced to a Periodic Optimization problem.

For this purpose, let $x_i(t)$ be the number of initiations of node i up to and including time t so that

$$b_{ij}(\sigma_j^k) = d_{ij} + x_i(\sigma_j^k - t_{ij}) - x_j(\sigma_j^k) + 1 .$$

Thus, if $r = k - d_{ij}$, one obtains

$$b_{ij}(\sigma_j^k) - 1 = b_{ij}\left(\sigma_j^{r+d_{ij}}\right) - 1 = d_{ij} + x_i\left(\sigma_j^{r+d_{ij}} - t_{ij}\right) - x_j\left(\sigma_j^{r+d_{ij}}\right) + 1 - 1 =$$

$$= d_{ij} + x_i\left(\sigma_j^{r+d_{ij}} - t_{ij}\right) - r - d_{ij} = x_i\left(\sigma_j^{r+d_{ij}} - t_{ij}\right) - r .$$

Therefore, from eq. (7.2) it follows that a necessary and sufficient condition for the feasibility of a schedule S is

$$x_i\left(\sigma_j^{r+d_{ij}} - t_{ij}\right) \geqslant r$$

which can be rewritten as

$$(7.4) \qquad \sigma_j^{r+d_{ij}} - t_{ij} \geqslant \sigma_i^r .$$

But, in a periodic schedule of period T, $\sigma_j^{r+d_{ij}} = t_j + (r + d_{ij})T$ and $\sigma_i^r = t_i + rT$;

hence, eq. (7.4) becomes

$$t_i - t_j - T d_{ij} \leqslant t_{ij} \, . \tag{7.5}$$

In conclusion, problem (7.3) consists in finding the minimum value of T (i.e., the maximum value of -T) for which the linear inequalities (7.5) can be satisfied. But this is exactly the Linear Programming formulation (4.8) of the following Periodic Optimization problem

$$\min_{\gamma \in E} \frac{\sum\limits_{\gamma} t_{ij}}{\sum\limits_{\gamma} d_{ij}} \tag{7.6}$$

Therefore, if problem (7.6) is solved by means of Algorithm 3.1 or 4.1, the minimum period T_m is found together with the optimal schedule P_{T_m} since the times t_i coincide with the "potentials" v_i of these algorithms.

In the numerical example considered above, one obtains, for example,

$$\gamma^0 = (1,2,7,8,1) \quad T_m = \frac{11}{2}$$

while a set of potentials (an optimal schedule) is given by

$$(v_i) = (t_i) = \left(0,3,0, \, -\frac{3}{2}, \, -\frac{1}{2}, 3, \, -\frac{3}{2}, \frac{3}{2} \right) .$$

(c) **A transportation problem**

A transportation problem is now described where one of the algorithms described in this chapter must be used as a subroutine in order to generate the column of coefficients needed in the solution of a large scale linear program (for more details see Dantzig, et. al. [7]).

Suppose there are n ports labelled from 1 to n and that amounts b_{ij} are required to be shipped from port i to port j. The shipping can either be done by charter at a cost v_{ij} per unit shipped or by using one of a fleet of m vessels under the control of the company.

Let us assign to the k-th vessel of the fleet a particular sequence of ports forming a cycle (in general not elementary) and let decompose this cycle in a set of elementary cycles $\gamma \in E$. Moreover, let g be an index ordering the elementary cycles. Thus a material balance for every arc (i,j) gives

$$y_{ij} + \sum_k \sum_g a_{kg}^{ij} x_{kg} = b_{ij} \tag{7.7}$$

where y_{ij} is the amount chartered from i to j, a_{kg}^{ij} is the amount carried from i to j by the k-th vessel of the fleet when it is on the g-th cycle (obviously $a_{kg}^{ij} = 0$ if (i,j) is not an arc of the g-th cycle) and x_{kg} is the number of times that the ship k is employed in the g-th cycle (fractional values of x_{kg} can be interpreted as rate of use of the ship in some given period of time).

Now, let h_k be the hours available on the k-th vessel, t_{kg} the time required by vessel k to complete the g-th cycle and s_k be the unused hours of the ship, during which the company makes a profit of $c_k s_k$ since we assume that the ship is operated by another company. Thus, for any vessel k of the fleet one has

(7.8)
$$\sum_g t_{kg} x_{kg} + s_k = h_k \qquad k = 1, \dots, m$$

and the objective function to be minimized is

(7.9)
$$z = \sum_{i,j} v_{ij} y_{ij} - \sum_k c_k s_k = \min .$$

Problem (7.6)-(7.9) is a Linear Programming problem which could be solved once all the coefficients are known. Unfortunately, in practical applications the number of different cycles is so high that the problem can be solved only by generating the column of the coefficients as needed, and by using y_{ij} and s_k as basic variables to get a first basic feasible solution (no vessel of the fleet is used). If p_{ij} and q_k are the simplex multipliers associated with eqs. (7.7) and (7.8), one needs to "price out" the column associated with x_{kg} and to find that column g for each vessel k that prices out most negative. The relative cost coefficient of x_{kg} that we must minimize is given by

(7.10)
$$-q_k t_{kg} - \sum_{i,j} p_{ij} a_{kg}^{ij} .$$

But, since a_{kg}^{ij} is the ship's capacity w_{ij}^k if (i,j) is in the g-th cycle γ_g and zero otherwise, the sum in eq. (7.10) is simply the sum of the ship capacities on arcs (i,j) weighted by p_{ij}, so that the relative cost coefficient of x_{kg} given by eq. (7.10) can be given the form

$$-q_k t_{kg} - \sum_{\gamma_g} p_{ij} w_{ij}^k .$$

Now, if we set $x_{kg} = \bar{x}_{kg} / t_{kg}$, the relative cost coefficients for the new problem are, obviously

$$-q_k - \frac{\sum_{\gamma_g} p_{ij} w_{ij}^k}{t_{kg}} \quad .$$

But, since q_k does not depend upon γ_g and $t_{kg} = \sum_{\gamma_g} t_{ij}^k$, the subproblem one must actually solve is

$$\min_{\gamma_g \in E} \frac{\sum_{\gamma_g} p_{ij} w_{ij}^k}{\sum_{\gamma_g} t_{ij}^k} \quad k = 1, \dots, m.$$

Thus, in conclusion, the solution of the Linear Programming problem (7.7)-(7.9) can be carried out by solving at each step a number of Periodic Optimization problems which equals the number of the ships in the fleet. The advantage of this method, which is, actually, a variant of the decomposition principle, is that it reduces the solution of a large Linear Programming problem to the solution of subproblems of lower complexity.

REFERENCES

[1]   I.V. Romanovskii, "Optimization of Stationary Control of a Discrete
        Deterministic Process" Kibernetica, vol. 3, n.2, pp. 66-78, March-
        -April 1967 (American translation in "Cybernetics").

[2]   I.L. Traiger and A. Gill, "On an Asymptotic Optimization Problem in Finite ,
        Directed, Weighted Graphs" Information and Control, vol. 13, n. 6 ,
        pp. 527-533, Dec. 1968.

[3]   S. Rinaldi, "Asymptotic Properties of the Cost Functions Associated to Any
        Infinite Path in a Finite Graph" 11th Int. Autom. and Instrum.
        Conf., Milano (Italy), Nov. 1970, published by Mondadori, Milano,
        Italy.

[4]   R. Howard, "Dynamic Programming and Markov Processes" Technology
        Press and Wiley, 1960.

[5]   R. Howard, "Dynamic Probabilistic Models" Volume II, John Wiley and
        Sons, 1971.

[6]   A. Fillières, "Cycles with Minimum Average Length" Report n.67-21 of the
        Operations Research Center, University of California, Berkeley, June
        1967.

[7]   G.B. Dantzig, W.O. Blattner and M.R. Rao "Finding a Cycle in a Graph with
        Minimum Cost to Time Ratio with Application to a Ship Routing
        Problem" Theory of Graphs, Int. Symp., Roma, Italy, July 1966,
        published by Dunod, Paris and Gordon and Breach, N.Y., pp. 77-83.

[8]   E.L. Lawler, "Optimal Cycles in Doubly Weighted Directed Linear Graphs"
        Theory of Graphs, Int. Symp., Roma, Italy, July 1966, published by
        Dunod, Paris and Gordon and Breach, N.Y., pp. 209-213.

[9]   R. Bellman, "Functional Equations in the Theory of Dynamic Programming, XI—Limit Theorems" Rend. Circolo Mat. Palermo, vol. 8, n. 3, pp. 343-345, 1959.

[10]   A. Kaufman and R. Cruon, "Dynamic Programming" Academic Press, New York, 1967.

[11]   S. Rinaldi and P. Rozzoni, "Iterative Methods in Function Space for the Optimization of Markov Chains" Ricerca Operativa, n.2, pp. 35-37, April 1971 (in Italian).

[12]   P. Dorato, "Steady State Optimal Control of Finite-State Machines" Automatica (IFAC Journal), vol. 7, n.3, pp. 351-358, May 1971.

[13]   B. Fox, "Finding Minimal Cost-Time Ratio Circuits" Operations Research, vol. 17, n. 3, pp. 546-550, May-June 1969.

[14]   G.B. Dantzig, "Linear Programming and Extensions" Princeton University Press, Princeton, N.J., 1963.

[15]   J.Y. Yen, "On the Efficiencies of Algorithms for Detecting Negative Loops in Networks" Santa Clara Business Review, University of Santa Clara, California, vol. 2, n.1, pp. 52-58, 1971.

[16]   J.Y. Yen, "An Algorithm for Finding Shortest Routes from All Source Nodes to Given Destination in General Networks" Quart. Appl. Math., vol. 27, n. 4, pp. 526-530, Jan. 1970.

[17]   F. Shapiro, "Shortest Route Methods for Finite State Space Dynamic Programming Problems" SIAM J. Applied Math., vol. 16, pp. 1232-1250, 1968.

[18]   R. Aris, G.L. Nemhauser and D.J. Wilde, "Optimization of Multistage Cyclic and Branching Systems by Serial Procedures" AIChE J., vol. 10, n. 6, pp. 913-919, Nov. 1964.

[19]   U. Bertelè and F. Brioschi, "Non Serial Dynamic Programming" Academic Press, New York, 1973.

[20]   R.A. Cunningham-Green, "Describing Industrial Processes with Interference and Approximating their Steady-State Behavior." Operational Research Quarterly, vol. 13, pp. 95-100, 1965.

[21]   R. Reiter, "Scheduling Parallel Computations" J. of ACM, vol. 15, n. 4, pp. 590-599, Oct. 1968.

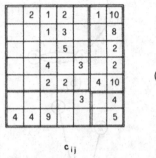

c_{ij}

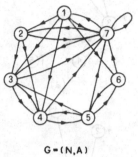

$G = (N, A)$

Fig. 2.1

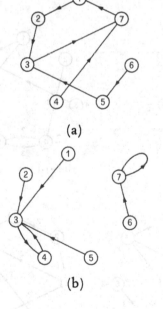

(a)

(b)

Fig. 3.1

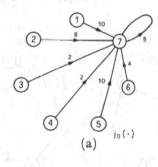

(a) $j_0(\cdot)$

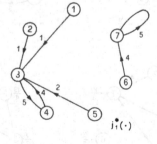

$j_1^*(\cdot)$

Fig. 3.2

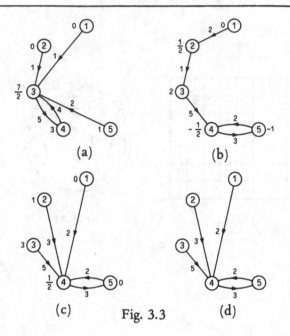

(a)

(b)

(c)   Fig. 3.3   (d)

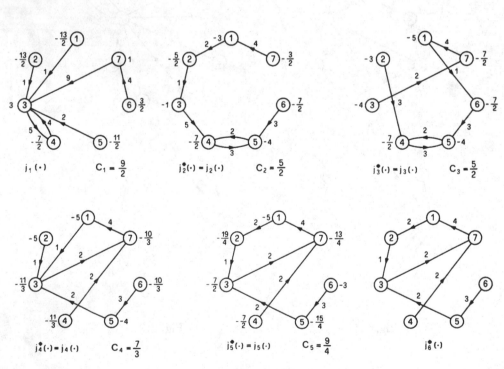

$j_1(\cdot)$ $C_1 = \dfrac{9}{2}$ $j_2^*(\cdot) = j_2(\cdot)$ $C_2 = \dfrac{5}{2}$ $j_3^*(\cdot) = j_3(\cdot)$ $C_3 = \dfrac{5}{2}$

$j_4^*(\cdot) = j_4(\cdot)$ $C_4 = \dfrac{7}{3}$ $j_5^*(\cdot) = j_5(\cdot)$ $C_5 = \dfrac{9}{4}$ $j_6^*(\cdot)$

Fig. 3.4

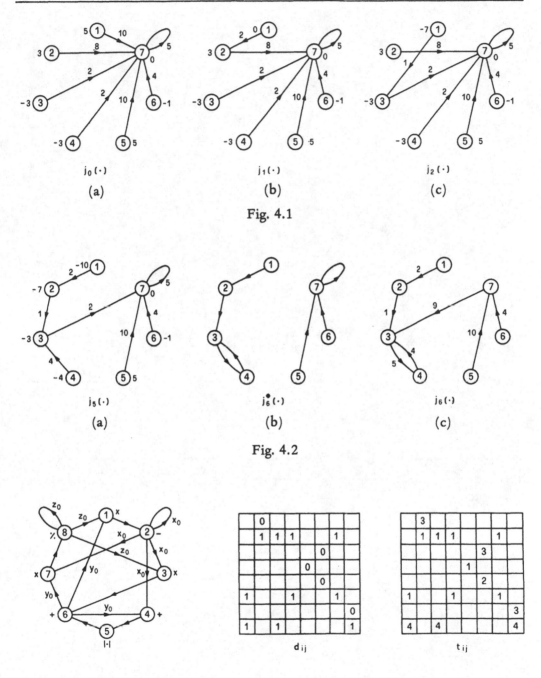

$j_0(\cdot)$

(a)

$j_1(\cdot)$

(b)

$j_2(\cdot)$

(c)

Fig. 4.1

$j_5(\cdot)$

(a)

$j_6^{\bullet}(\cdot)$

(b)

$j_6(\cdot)$

(c)

Fig. 4.2

Fig. 7.1

d_{ij}

t_{ij}

Fig. 7.2

OPTIMAL CONSTRAINED CYCLES IN GRAPHS (*)

S. Rinaldi(**)

1. INTRODUCTION

This chapter is devoted to the study of some constrained Periodic Optimization problems which have been considered in the literature.

Unfortunately, these problems are not so simple as the unconstrained one, (see the preceding Chapter) since the optimal cycle is not, in general, an elementary cycle. Moreover, for some of the problems one has also to worry about the existence of the solution.

Two types of constraints are considered in the following: path constraints (see Sects. 2 and 3) and integral constraints (see Sects. 4-7) and in each one of the two cases the effort is toward identifying some structural properties of the optimal solution which recall the elementarity property of the unconstrained case.

Thus, the optimal solution of the problem with path constraints is shown to be constituted by a cycle which is elementary in certain specified nodes, while the optimal cycle for the case of integral constraints can be decomposed in special elementary cycles (called basic cycles) and the number of these cycles is simply related with the number of constraints.

These properties are very important since they allow handling of the problems by means of very simple algorithms, which can be interpreted as generalizations of two of the algorithms presented for the solution of the unconstrained case.

(*) This work has been supported by Centro Teoria dei Sistemi, C.N.R., Milano, Italy.

(**) Istituto di Elettrotecnica ed Elettronica del Politecnico di Milano, Italy.

2. PROBLEMS WITH PATH CONSTRAINTS

A Periodic Optimization problem with path constraints is one where the optimal cycle is constrained to meet at least one node of a given subset X_0 of the nodes.

In other words this corresponds to consider as feasible cycles only those cycles which have at least one node in common with X_0.

A particular problem of this type is obtained in the limit case $X_0 = \{\bar{x}_0\}$, namely when the optimal cycle is forced to pass through a given node of the graph, say node 1.

An optimal solution to this constrained Periodic Optimization problem does not, in general, exist if the length $\tau(\gamma) = \sum_{\gamma} t_{ij}$ of the cycle γ is not constrained. In fact, suppose that node 1 does not belong to any cycle γ_{unc}^0 which is the optimal solution of the unconstrained problem, and consider the non-elementary cycle $\gamma^{(k)}$ constituted by a path from node 1 to node i* of γ_{unc}^0, followed by the cycle γ_{unc}^0 repeated k times and by a path from i* to i (recall that such paths exist because the graph is, by assumption, strongly connected). Since, $\lim_{k \to \infty} C(\gamma^{(k)}) = C_{unc}^0$ and $C(\gamma^{(k)}) > C_{unc}^0$ for all k, obviously, the path constrained problem does not have an optimal solution if $\tau(\gamma)$ is unbounded.

Thus, the standard Periodic Optimization problem with path constraints that we shall consider in the following is to find the cycle passing through node 1 with minimum average cost and with length $\tau(\gamma)$ less than or equal to a maximum allowed length T.

This is the problem of the "married" traveling salesman who leaves in city 1 and would like to see his wife at least once a week, and, actually, this problem is a particular case of the "unmarried" traveling salesman problem who can visit n cities and has a girl friend in every one of the first r cities (r < n). Although his main interest is to maximize his profit, he is constraining himself to visit at least once a week one of the r "attractive" cities.

The reader could be, perhaps, more convinced about the importance of this problem, if he considers the following alternative situation (see Lawler [1], Locatelli et al. [2] and Lawler and Rinaldi [3]), which is a generalization of a transportation problem proposed by Dantzig. et al. [4].

A tramp steamer, is free to choose its ports of call and the order in which it calls on them. A voyage from port i to port j earns p_{ij} dollars profit and requires t_{ij} days times. There are only certain ports at which the steamer can refuel and a cycle must be found which is optimal, subject to the constraint that the travel time between two successive refuelings does not exceed a certain time T.

An abstract formulation of the problem is as follows.

Let $G = (N,A)$ be a finite directed graph where N is the set of nodes (ports) and A is the set of arcs. A "cost" $c_{ij} \lessgtr 0$ and a "transit time" $t_{ij} > 0$ are assigned to every arc $(i,j) \epsilon A$ (the weights c_{ij} and t_{ij} are integer numbers and $|c_{ij}| \leqslant \alpha$, $t_{ij} \leqslant \tau$).

The set N is partitioned into the subset R (refueling ports) and N−R (non-refueling ports), with cardinalities r and n-r respectively. Let

$$\tau(\gamma) = \sum_{\gamma} t_{ij}$$

and

$$\mathcal{C}(\gamma) = \sum_{\gamma} c_{ij}$$

be the "length" and the "cost" of any path γ in the graph.

A finite path γ can be decomposed in an obvious way into a sequence of paths which, besides the initial and (or) final nodes, do not pass through any node of R. In the following, a path γ is said to be feasible if the length of any subpath of this sequence is less than or equal to a given positive integer T (maximum running time).

If F is the set of all feasible cycles (elementary or not) in the graph and

$$C(\gamma) = \frac{\mathcal{C}(\gamma)}{\tau(\gamma)}$$

is the "average cost" of any cycle $\gamma \epsilon F$, then the following optimization problem is of interest. Find $\gamma^o \epsilon F$ such that

$$c^o \triangleq C(\gamma^o) \triangleq \min_{\gamma \epsilon F} C(\gamma).$$

A first trivial though important remark consists in noticing that "at least one optimal cycle (if any) is contained in the finite set E of all feasible cycles which are elementary in the refueling nodes", i.e.,

$$c^o = \min_{\gamma \epsilon E} C(\gamma). \tag{2.1}$$

Moreover, since

$$\tau(\gamma) \leqslant rT \qquad \forall \gamma \in E$$

the following property holds

$$(2.2) \quad |C(\gamma_1) - C(\gamma_2)| \geqslant \frac{1}{r^2 T^2} \qquad \forall \gamma_1, \gamma_2 \in E : C(\gamma_1) \neq C(\gamma_2).$$

Therefore, if (a,b) is an interval of uncertainty of the optimal average cost C^o(i.e., $a \leqslant C^o \leqslant b$) and $b-a < 1/r^2 T^2$, then all the cycles $\gamma \in E$ such that $C(\gamma) \in (a,b)$ are optimal cycles. This property will be used in the next section in order to define the end test of an iterative procedure and to bound the number of iterations required by such a procedure.

3.A BINARY SEARCH PROCEDURE

The problem stated in the preceding section can be solved following the idea presented in Section 5 for the unconstrained problem.

In fact, if the new costs

$$\bar{c}_{ij}(C) = c_{ij} - Ct_{ij}$$

are associated to every arc $(i,j) \in A$, one of the following three situations must , a priori, hold.

Case 1   There exists a cycle $\gamma \in E$ which is negative w.r.t. $\bar{c}_{ij}(C)$.

Case 2   All cycles $\gamma \in E$ are positive w.r.t. $\bar{c}_{ij}(C)$.

Case 3   All cycles $\gamma \in E$ are non-negative w.t.r. $\bar{c}_{ij}(C)$ and there is a cycle $\gamma \in E$ which is a zero-cost cycle.

Again, in Case 1 $C^o \leqslant C(\gamma) < C$, while in Case 2 $C < C^o$ and in Case 3 $C = C^o$. Therefore, a monotonic or a binary search procedure for the determination of γ^o and C^o can easily be devised, if one has a way for testing the existence of negative cycles in the set E.

This operation can actually be accomplished first by computing the weights

$f_{ij}(C) \triangleq$ the cost ($\Sigma \bar{c}_{ij}(C)$) of a least-costly feasible path from i to j $(i,j \in R)$ with the constraint that the path does not pass through any one of the refueling nodes (except initial and final nodes)

and then by testing for the existence of negative cycles in the complete graph which has the set R as set of nodes and the weights f_{ij} (C) associated with its arcs.

This test for negative cycles can be accomplished by means of the procedure described in Section 5 of chapter 2 and the complexity of the computation is $O(r^3)$ additions and comparisons. By means of eq. (2.2) one can prove that if the monotonic search is used the number of iterations needed in the worst possible case is $2\alpha T^2 r^2$ while this number is only $1 + \log_2 \alpha + 2\log_2 r + 2\log_2 T$ for a binary search procedure. Thus, only the binary search is here described, although the monotonic search procedure seems to work well in practice (see example below).

Algorithm 3.1.

1.   Let a $\leqslant C^o \leqslant$ b (for example a $= -\alpha$, b $= \alpha$).
2.   If b-a $\leqslant 1/r^2 T^2$, put C = b and go to 4. Otherwise go to 3.
3.   Let C $= (a + b)/2$ be an estimate of C^o.
4.   Evaluate $\bar{c}_{ij}$ (C) $= c_{ij} - Ct_{ij}$.
5.   Compute f_{ij} (C), i,j $\in$ R.
6.   Test for negative cycles w.r.t. f_{ij}(C) in the complete graph which has
          the set R as set of nodes
          If Case 1 holds let b = C and go to 2.
          If Case 2 holds let a = C and go to 2.
          If Case 3 holds C^o = C. Stop.

Two different recursive equations for the computation of the weights f_{ij} (C) defined above are now described. For the sake of simplicity in notation, the parameter C will not be explicitly mentioned from now on so that for example f_{ij} will stand for f_{ij} (C).

Let

f_{ij} (t) $\triangleq$ the cost ($\Sigma \bar{c}_{ij}$) of a least-costly path from i to j (i,j $\in$ N) with the constraints that the path is of length less than or equal to t ($\Sigma t_{ij} \leqslant t$) and does not pass through any one of the refueling nodes (except initial and (or) final nodes).

Of course $f_{ij} = f_{ij}$ (T).

First Method

Let

$$f_{ij}(t) = \infty \quad \forall t \leqslant 0.$$

Then, by standard dynamic programming, one obtains

$$f_{ij}(t) = \begin{cases} \min\limits_{k \in N-R} (f_{ik}(t - t_{kj}) + \bar{c}_{kj}) & t < t_{ij} \\ \min\limits_{ij} [\bar{c}_{ij}; \min\limits_{k \in N-R} (f_{ik}(t - t_{kj}) + \bar{c}_{kj})] & t \geqslant t_{ij} . \end{cases}$$

Since $i \epsilon R$, $j \epsilon N$, $k \epsilon N-R$ and $t = 1,2,...,T$, the complexity of this method is $O(rn(n-r)T)$ and has the characteristic of not depending upon τ.

A second method also based upon dynamic programming can be obtained if the decomposition of an optimal path into two subpaths is carried out in a different way.

Let $\lfloor a \rfloor$ be the greatest integer less than or equal to a and $\lceil a \rceil$ the least integer greater that or equal to a. Thus, a path of length t can be decomposed into two paths with lengths not exceeding $\lfloor t/2 \rfloor - \delta$ and $\lceil t/2 \rceil + \delta$, for some δ such that $0 \leqslant \delta \leqslant \tau$. Hence the following successive equations can be understood (note that $\lceil t/2 \rceil + \delta \geqslant t$ implies $\lfloor t/2 \rfloor - \delta \leqslant 0$).

Second Method

$$f_{ij}(t) = \infty \quad \forall t \leqslant 0$$

$$f_{ij}(t) = \begin{cases} \min\limits_{\delta} \min\limits_{k \in N-R} \left[f_{ik}(\lfloor t/2 \rfloor - \delta) + f_{kj}(\lceil t/2 \rceil + \delta) \right] & t < t_{ij} \\ \min\limits_{\delta} \left\{ \bar{c}_{ij}; \min\limits_{k \in N-R} \left[f_{ik}(\lfloor t/2 \rfloor - \delta) + f_{kj}(\lceil t/2 \rceil + \delta) \right] \right\} & t \geqslant t_{ij} . \end{cases}$$

Now define

$$S^{(i)} = \left\{ t : a^{(i)} \leqslant t \leqslant b^{(i)}, \quad t = \text{integer} \right\}$$

and

$$a^{(1)} = b^{(1)} = T$$

$$a^{(i)} = \lfloor a^{(i-1)}/2 \rfloor - \tau \qquad b^{(i)} = \lceil b^{(i-1)}/2 \rceil + \tau.$$

Moreover, let h be the minimum integer i such that

$$0 \in S^{(i)}$$

and let

$$S = \bigcup_{i=1}^{h} S^{(i)}.$$

Since $f_{ij}(t)$ can be computed from the values $f_{ij}(\xi)$ for

$$\xi \in \left[\lfloor t/2 \rfloor - \tau, \ \lceil t/2 \rceil + \tau \right]$$

the recursive equations must be solved for $t \in S$ and $i \in N$, $j \in N$, $k \in N\text{-}R$. Hence, the complexity of this method is $O(n^2(n-r)\tau \mid S \mid)$ where $\mid S \mid$ is the cardinality of S. The cardinality of $S^{(i)}$ is bounded by 4τ, while h is less than or equal to $\lceil \log_2 T/\tau \rceil$ since $T/2^h - \tau \leqslant 0$ implies $h \geqslant \log_2 T/\tau$. Thus, this method is $O(4n^2(n-r)\tau^2 \log_2 T/\tau)$ in complexity.

In conclusion, the number of iterations required by the algorithm is bounded by $1 + \log_2 \alpha + 2\log_2 r + 2\log_2 T$, while the total number of elementary operations involved in every iteration (Steps 4, 5 and 6 of the algorithm) is bounded by

$$n^2 + V(r,n,\tau,T) + r^3$$

where $V(r, n, \tau, T)$ represents the number of operations required for the computation of the weights $f_{ij}(C)$. The first method proposed gives

$$V(r,n,\tau,T) = rn(n-r)T$$

while the second one gives

$$V(r,n,\tau,T) = 4n^2(n-r)\tau^2 \log_2 T/\tau.$$

Thus, method 1 should be used when

$$\frac{r}{n} < \frac{4\tau}{(T/\tau)/(\log_2 T/\tau)},$$

while Method 2 seems to be preferable in all other cases. In particular, when the following inequality on the "time" parameters holds

$$(3.1) \qquad\qquad 4\tau > \frac{T/\tau}{\log_2 T/\tau}$$

Method 1 seems to have some advantage in the order of complexity.

Example 3.1.

Consider the finite graph with n = 5 described in Fig. 3.1. and suppose r = 1 (the only refueling node is node 1) and T = 23.

Since τ = 5, eq. (3.1) is satisfied; therefore, the first method is used for the computation of f_{11} (C).

Moreover, in this case Step 6 of the algorithm reduces to test for the sign of f_{11} (T). Of course, if f_{11} (t) < 0 for some t < T, the recursive equations of Method 1 can be stopped since there is a feasible negative cycle of length t passing through node 1.

In the problem at hand, a first interval of uncertainty is, for example, a = 0, b = 5. Thus, the first trial value is C = 5 and using Method 1 one gets f_{11} (6) < 0. Therefore, the second trial value is c = 2.5, and, again, Method 1 detects a negative cycle. Proceeding this way, after 15 iterations one obtains the optimal non-elementary cycle γ^o = (1,4,3,4,3,2,1) of length $\tau(\gamma^o)$ = 22 and cost C^o = 3/11.

Of course, this example can also be worked out by applying the monotonic search, namely by determining, at every step, a negative cycle γ by means of Method 1 and then by assuming as a new value of C the average cost C(γ) of such a cycle. If this is the case, the optimal solution is obtained in six iterations as shown in Fig. 3.2.

This means that although the number of iterations required by the monotonic search in the worst possible case is greater than the one required by the binary search ($2\alpha T^2 r^2 \gg 1 + \log_2 \alpha + 2\log_2 r + 2\log_2 T$) it can happen that for the actual number of iterations the relation is just the opposite. This situation has been checked to be very frequent, in practical cases, where the number of iterations required by the monotonic search is often incomparably less than the bound $2\alpha T^2 r^2$ (for example, in the problem at hand $2\alpha T^2 r^2$ = 5290 while the actual number of iterations is 6).   □

4. PROBLEMS WITH INTEGRAL CONSTRAINTS

A different kind of problem one can encounter in applications is the so-called Periodic Optimization problem with integral constraints, that is dealt with from now on (see Locatelli et al. [2] and [5]).

This is the case when q "constraint values" v_{ij}^k , k = 1, . . . ,q, are associated to each arc (i,j) of the graph G = (N,A) and a cycle γ is said to be feasible when the "constraint rates"

$$v^k(\gamma) \triangleq \frac{V^{\cdot k}(\gamma)}{\tau(\gamma)} \triangleq \frac{\sum_\gamma v_{ij}^k}{\sum_\gamma t_{ij}}$$

satisfy some equality or inequality relations, of the kind

$$v^k(\gamma) \geqslant \bar{v}^k \qquad k = 1,\ldots,q. \qquad (4.1)$$

In practical applications, $\bar{v}^k$ can represent a desired consumption or production rate of good k. For example, consider again our traveling salesman and suppose he is selling products of q different makes. Unfortunately, he is not free to choose any policy for selling his goods, since he must sell, on the average, at least a certain amount $\bar{V}^k$ of products of make k. Thus, his problem is to determine among the cycles satisfying eq. (4.1) that cycle γ^o which maximizes his average profit or, in other words, minimizes his average cost, i.e.,

$$c^o \triangleq C(\gamma^o) = \min_\gamma C(\gamma) = \min_\gamma \frac{\mathcal{C}(\gamma)}{\tau(\gamma)}. \qquad (4.2)$$

This problem is, obviously, not so simple as the unconstrained problem, since, unfortunately, the nice structural property of the optimal cycle γ^o being elementary does not hold any more. Nevertheless, the optimal solution of this problem can be shown (see next section) to be essentially constituted by q + 1 elementary cycles (basic cycles), which actually can be determined by means of an extension of the Linear Programming method presented for the unconstrained problem.

5. BASIC CYCLES AND THE EXISTENCE PROBLEM

The existence of the optimal solution of the problem of Periodic Optimization with integral constraints is discussed in this section from a geometrical point of view. For the sake of simplicity, only the case of equality constraints

$$V^k (\gamma) = \vec{V}^k \qquad k = 1, \ldots, q$$

is dealt with, while the obvious extension to the case of inequalities is left to the reader (see, also, Section 7).

Let $\gamma_1, \ldots, \gamma_K$ be all the elementary cycles in the graph and associate to each cycle γ_i its loss rate $C_i \triangleq C(\gamma_i)$ and its q "constraint rates" $V_i^k \triangleq V^k(\gamma_i)$, $k = 1, \ldots, q$. Thus K points $Z_1, \ldots, Z_K$ representing the loss and constraint rates of all elementary cycles of the graph can be located in the $(q + 1)$-dimensional vector space $V^1 \times V^2 \times \ldots V^q \times C$ (see Fig. 5.1).

Now, observe that each cycle γ (in general non-elementary) can be decomposed, in an obvious way, into elementary cycles γ_i each one repeated m_i times (the non-negative integer m_i is called the "multiplicity" of the i-th elementary cycle γ_i). For example, the cycle

$$\gamma = (1,3,4,3,4,3,4,2,1,5,1)$$

is decomposed in three elementary cycles

$$\gamma_1 = (1,3,4,2,1) \quad \gamma_2 = (3,4,3) \quad \gamma_3 = (1,5,1)$$

of multiplicity $m_1 = 1$, $m_2 = 2$ and $m_3 = 1$. Of course, an "assignment" $m = (m_1, \ldots, m_k)$ of non-negative integers does not always correspond to a cycle γ, since, for this to be true, a certain kind of connectivity property must, obviously, be satisfied. For example, if $\gamma_1 = (1,2,1)$ and $\gamma_2 = (4,5,4)$, the assignment $m = (1,1,0, \ldots, 0)$ corresponds to the union of two disconnected cycles. In the following, such assignments are called "acyclic" while all the others are called "cyclic".

Note that since the graph is strongly connected one can always find a cycle γ_{conn} (in general non-elementary) which connects any set of disconnected cycles corresponding to an acyclic assignment, or, in other words, any acyclic assignment $m = (m_1, \ldots, m_K)$ can always be modified into a cyclic one $\bar{m} = (\bar{m}_1, \ldots, \bar{m}_K)$ with $\bar{m}_i = m_i$ if $m_i > 0$ and $\bar{m}_i = 0,1$ if $m_i = 0$. Finally, it must be noted that many cycles are, in general, associated to a cyclic assignment. Nevertheless, all these cycles have the same loss rate and constraint rates since they contain the same arcs, each one repeated the same number of times. Therefore, from our point of view, they can be considered as a unique cycle.

Now, consider a cycle γ and its assignment $m = (m_1, \ldots, m_K)$ and write its average cost $C(\gamma)$ and its constraint rates $V^k(\gamma)$, $k = 1, \ldots, q$, as

$$C(\gamma) = \frac{\sum\limits_{i=1}^{K} m_i \, \ell(\gamma_i)}{\sum\limits_{i=1}^{K} m_i \, \tau(\gamma_i)}$$

$$V^k(\gamma) = \frac{\sum\limits_{i=1}^{K} m_i \, V^{\cdot k}(\gamma_i)}{\sum\limits_{i=1}^{K} m_i \, \tau(\gamma_i)} \qquad k = 1, \ldots, q.$$

By defining the coefficients

$$\lambda_i = \frac{m_i \, \tau(\gamma_i)}{\sum\limits_{i=1}^{K} m_i \, \tau(\gamma_i)} \qquad i = 1, \ldots, K \qquad (5.1)$$

one obtains

$$C(\gamma) = \sum_{i=1}^{K} \lambda_i \, C_i$$

$$V^k(\gamma) = \sum_{i=1}^{K} \lambda_i \, V_i^k \qquad k = 1, \ldots, q.$$

Since $0 \leqslant \lambda_i \leqslant 1$ and $\sum\limits_{i=1}^{K} \lambda_i = 1$, the cost and constraint rates of γ are a suitable convex combination of the C_i's and V_i^k's and the coefficients λ_i of the convex combination can be easily computed by means of eq. (5.1) once the assignment $m = (m_1, \ldots, m_K)$ corresponding to γ is known. Therefore, the polyedron P defined by the convex cover of the K points $Z_1, \ldots, Z_K$ (see Fig. 5.1) contains the set of all loss and constraint rates which can be obtained with non-elementary cycles.

The coefficients λ_i defined by eq. (5.1) cannot, however, be arbitrary real numbers. Therefore, a cycle cannot, in general, be associated to each point of P, even if it can be obviously stated that in each neighborhood of such a point there is an infinity of points corresponding to non-elementary cycles. Thus, the existence of the optimal solution of the problem is guaranteed if there exists a cycle γ_A associated to the lower intersection A of the straight line $V^k = \bar{V}^k$, $k = 1, \ldots, q$ and the plyedron P (see Fig. 5.1).

Of course, if a cycle γ_A associated to the point A exists, then it can be decomposed into elementary cycles corresponding to the vertices of the face $\mathscr{F}_A^\cdot$ of P where the point A lies (see points Z_1, Z_2 and Z_3 of Fig. 5.1). These elementary cycles, say $\gamma_1, \ldots, \gamma_r$ and any corresponding assignment m = { $m_1 \ldots, m_r : 0, \ldots ,0$ } are called "basic" so that our final statement is as follows.

Proposition 5.1

An optimal cycle γ^o (if any) can be decomposed into basic cycles.   □

Therefore, if the basic cycles are pairwise disconnected, i.e., if any non-trivial basic assignment is acyclic, no optimal solution can exist to the problem. Of course, this is only a sufficient condition for the non-existence of the optimal solution.

Something more precise can be said when all the data of the problem (c_{ij}, t_{ij}, v_{ij}^k, $\bar{V}^k$) are integer numbers. In fact, in such a case, the point A has rational coordinates which can be given the form of a convex combination — with rational coefficients λ_i^A — of the coordinates of the vertices of $\mathscr{F}_A^\cdot$, i.e.,

with
$$\lambda_i^A = \frac{m_i^A}{M} \qquad m_i^A = \text{non-negative integer}$$
$$m_i^A = 0 \qquad \text{for } i = r+1, \ldots, K$$

and
$$\sum_{i=1}^{r} m_i^A = M.$$

A basic assignment $m^A = (m_1^A, \ldots, m_r^A, 0, \ldots, 0)$ is associated in this way to the point A and if such a basic assignment is cyclic an optimal solution exists.

In order to conclude our discussion and motivate the next section, we now state that the determination of the basic assignment m^A is of great interest even if the problem does not have a solution (i.e., even if m^A is acyclic).

In fact, if the operator "min" is replaced by the "weaker" operator "inf" in problem (4.1), (4.2), i.e.,

$$C^o = \inf C(\gamma)$$

subject to

$$v^k(\gamma) = \bar{v}^k,$$

the values C^o of the performance and $\bar{V}^k$ of the constraints can be approximated at will by means of a cycle γ^* which can be easily derived from the basic assignment m^A.

The cycle γ^* can be determined as follows. Given the basic assignment $m^A = (m_1^A, \ldots, m_r^A, 0, \ldots, 0)$ which is by assumption acyclic, consider the assignment $\bar{m}^A = (hm_1^A, \ldots, hm_r^A, 0, \ldots, 0)$, h positive interger, which is also basic and acyclic and transform it in a cyclic assignment m^* by adding a connecting cycle γ_{conn} constituted by a few elementary cycles γ_i with multiplicity $m_i = 1$. The cycle γ^* associated to m^* has an average cost $C(\gamma^*)$ given by

$$C(\gamma^*) = \frac{\mathcal{C}(\gamma_{conn}) + h \sum_{i=1}^{r} m_i \mathcal{C}(\gamma_i)}{\tau(\gamma_{conn}) + h \sum_{i=1}^{r} m_i \tau(\gamma_i)}$$

so that

$$\lim_{h \to \infty} C(\gamma^*) = C^o,$$

and the same result hods for $V^k(\gamma^*)$. Thus, the average cost C^o and the constraint $\bar{V}^k$ can be approximated at will provided h is large enough. In other words, the basic cycles $\gamma_1, \ldots, \gamma_r$ must be run a sufficiently high number of times so that the connecting cycle γ_{conn} has a negligible influence on the loss and constraint rates.

Finally, since the convex polyedron P belongs to a (q + 1)- dimensional vector space, the point A can be expressed as the convex combination of at most $q + 1$ vertices of $\mathcal{F}_A^*$. This implies that C^o and $\bar{V}^k$ can always be approximated by means of a non-elementary cycle constituted by at most $q + 1$ basic cycles and (eventually) a "connecting" cycle.

6. A LINEAR PROGRAMMING ALGORITHM FOR FINDING BASIC CYCLES

A Linear Programming algorithm for finding a basic assignment m^A and the corresponding basic cycles is now presented.

As it has been pointed out in the previous section, our constrained Periodic Optimization problem admits a solution if this assignment is cyclic, while, in the other case, the average cost C^o and the constraint rates $\bar{V}^k$ of problem

$$C^o = \inf_{\gamma} C(\gamma)$$

subject to

$$v^k(\gamma) = \vec{v}^k$$

can be approximated at will by a non-elementary cycle γ^* which can be easily derived from the basic assignment m^A.

Now, consider the following integer programming formulation of our problem (4.1), (4.2):

(6.1a)
$$\min_{x_{ij}} \frac{\sum_{i,j} c_{ij} x_{ij}}{\sum_{i,j} t_{ij} x_{ij}}$$

subject to

(6.1b)
$$\sum_i x_{ij} = \sum_k x_{jk} \qquad\qquad j = 1,\ldots,n$$

(6.1c)
$$\frac{\sum_{i,j} v_{ij}^{(k)} x_{ij}}{\sum_{i,j} t_{ij} x_{ij}} = \vec{v}^{(k)}, \qquad k = 1,\ldots,q$$

(6.1d)
$$x_{ij} = \text{non-negative integer}, \quad i,j = 1,\ldots,n$$

and assume the problem has an optimal solution x_{ij}^o. Thus, the basic assignment $m^A = (m_1^A,\ldots,m_2^A, 0,\ldots,0)$ and the basic cycles $\gamma_1,\ldots,\gamma_r$ can be obtained by applying the following procedure, which does not need to be proved.

Procedure 6.1.

Let $x_{ij}^{(1)} = x_{ij}^{(o)}$ and

(6.2)
$$m_1^A = \min_{i,j}\left(x_{ij}^{(1)} \mid x_{ij}^{(1)} > 0\right)$$

Moreover, let (i_1, i_2) be the first arc in the lexicographic ordering such that

$$x_{i_1 i_2}^{(1)} = m_1^A.$$

Then determine the arc (i_2, i_3) so that

(6.3)
$$x_{i_2 i_3}^{(1)} = \min_j\left(x_{i_2 j}^{(1)} \mid x_{i_2 j}^{(1)} > 0\right)$$

and continue this way until a cycle $\gamma_1 = (i_1, i_2, \ldots, i_l)$ is obtained. Thus, let

$$x_{ij}^{(2)} = \begin{cases} x_{ij}^{(1)} & \text{if } (i,j) \text{ does not belong to } \gamma_1 \\ x_{ij}^{(1)} - m_1 & \text{otherwise} \end{cases}$$

and reapply eqs. (6.2) and (6.3). A new cycle γ_2 and its associated multiplicity m_2^A are obtained.

By iteration, one gets a finite sequence of basic cycles $\gamma_1, \ldots, \gamma_r$ and a basic assignment $m^A = (m_1^A, \ldots, m_r^A, 0, \ldots, 0)$.

Now consider the following Linear Program

$$\min \sum_{i,j} c_{ij} y_{ij} \tag{6.4a}$$

subject to

$$\sum_i y_{ij} = \sum_k y_{ik}, \quad j = 1, \ldots, n \tag{6.4b}$$

$$\sum_{i,j} v_{ij} y_{ij} = \bar{v}^{(k)}, \quad k = 1, \ldots, q \tag{6.4c}$$

$$\sum_{i,j} t_{ij} y_{ij} = 1 \tag{6.4d}$$

$$y_{ij} \geq 0 \quad , \quad i,j = 1, \ldots, n. \tag{6.4e}$$

Since we assume that all data are integer numbers, an optimal solution y_{ij}^o of problem (6.4) can be given the form

$$y_{ij}^o = \frac{x_{ij}^o}{T} \tag{6.5}$$

where T is a positive integer and all x_{ij}^o are non-negative integers. Moreover, x_{ij}^o is an optimal solution of problem (6.1) (this can be proved following the same kind of reasoning used in Section 4 of chapter 2) so that the following algorithm for the determination of a basic assignment m^A is obtained.

Algorithm 6.1.

1.   Determine y_{ij}^o by solving the Linear Programming problem (6.4).

2.   Determine x_{ij}^o by putting y_{ij}^o in the form (6.5).
3.   Determine $\gamma_1, \ldots, \gamma_r$ and the basic assignment $m^A =$
            $= (m_1^A, \ldots, m_r^A, 0, \ldots 0)$ by applying Procedure 6.1 to x_{ij}^o.

Example 6.1.

Consider the finite system with $n = 3$ and $\overline{V} = 4$ described in Fig. 6.1, where the entries correspond to possible state transitions.

The solution of the Linear Program (6.4) is given by

$$y_{12}^o = y_{21}^o = \frac{1}{6}$$

$$y_{33}^o = \frac{2}{3}$$

$$y_{ij}^o = 0 \quad \text{for all other } (i, j).$$

Step 2 of the algorithm gives

$$y_{12}^o = \frac{x_{12}^o}{T} = \frac{1}{6}$$

$$y_{21}^o = \frac{x_{21}^o}{T} = \frac{1}{6}$$

$$y_{33}^o = \frac{x_{33}^o}{T} = \frac{4}{6}.$$

Thus, Procedure 6.1 can be applied. The first iteration gives

$$m_1^A = 1$$

$$x_{i_1 i_2}^{(1)} = x_{12}^{(1)}$$

$$x_{i_2 i_3}^{(1)} = x_{21}^{(1)}$$

i.e., $\gamma_1 = (1, 2, 1)$.
The second (and last) iteration gives

$$x_{33}^{(2)} = x_{33}^{(1)} = 4$$

$$x_{12}^{(2)} = x_{21}^{(2)} = 0$$

$$m_2^A = 4$$

$$x_{i_1 i_2}^{(2)} = x_{33}^{(2)}$$

i.e., $\gamma_2 = (3, 3)$.

Since γ_1 and γ_2 are disconnected, they do not constitute a cycle γ, and the problem does not have an optimal solution.

Nevertheless, the cost rate

$$c^o = \frac{m_1^A \mathcal{C}(\gamma_1) + m_2^A \mathcal{C}(\gamma_2)}{m_1^A \mathcal{T}(\gamma_1) + m_2^A \mathcal{T}(\gamma_2)} = \frac{5}{3}$$

and the constraint rate $\bar{V} = 4$ can be approximated at will by a cycle γ^* constituted by γ_1 run hm_1^A times, γ_2 run hm_2^A times and $\gamma_{conn} = (1, 2, 3,)$ run only once. For instance, $h = 100$ gives

$$c(\gamma^*) = \frac{1015}{605} = c^o + 0.01$$

$$v(\gamma^*) = \frac{2415}{605} = \bar{V} - 0.08.$$

7. EXAMPLE

An example of integral constrained Periodic Optimization can be derived from a particular production sequencing problem (see Locatelli et al. [2]).

The best cyclic operation of a plant for colouring artificial fibres must be found. The plant can simultaneously colour two fibres, so that if $k = 1, \ldots, q$ are the possible colours the system has $n = (1/2)q(q + 1)$ states (couples of colours) and the problem can be described on a complete graph with n nodes.

Let i_k be the node corresponding to treating both fibres with colour k and N_k be the set of nodes corresponding to only one of the fibres with colour k. When the process is working, 2v pounds of fiber are coloured in one unit of time, while there is, obviously, no production when setting up the machine. A profit p is made for every 2v pounds of coloured fibre and the rate of production of fibre of colour k must be greater than or equal to a certain prescribed amount V^k .

The determination of the best periodic schedule for such a problem consists in finding the cycle of maximum (minimum) average profit (cost) which satisfies the production requirements. The data t_{ij} , p_{ij} ($= -c_{ij}$) and v_{ij}^k are as follows

$$t_{ij} = \begin{cases} \text{positive integer} & i \neq j \text{ (time for setting up)} \\ \\ 1 & i = j \end{cases}$$

$$p_{ij} = \begin{cases} 0 & i \neq j \text{ (no profit is made when} \\ & \qquad\qquad\quad \text{setting up)} \\ p & i = j \end{cases}$$

$$v_{ij}^k = \begin{cases} 0 & i \neq j \text{ (no production is made when} \\ & \qquad\qquad\quad \text{setting up)} \\ 0 & i = j \notin X_k \cup i_k \\ v & i = j \in X_k \\ 2v & i = j = i_k \end{cases}$$

and the problem can be solved by means of Algorithm 6.1.

The particular structure of the data implies the optimal solution enjoys some special properties: at least one optimal solution is constituted by a number of basic cycles which equals the number of colours, and these basic cycles are all selfloops. The reason for such a property can be easily understood by the simple case: $q = 2$.

The situation is described in Fig. 7.1 where -C stands for profit.

The three selfloops of the graph correspond to the points Z_1 , Z_2 and Z_3 , while all other elementary cycles give rise to point Z_4 (no production and no profit). The polyedron P degenerates in the triangle $Z_1 Z_2 Z_4$ and all feasible solutions stay in the dashed triangle AXY. If the point Z_3 lies within the segment XY, an optimal solution exists since Z_3 is associated with a cycle (a selfloop); otherwise no point of the segment XY can represent a cycle since the three selfloops are disconnected; therefore the profit p can only be approximated (for example by means of a cycle γ^* constituted by the selfloops (1,1) and (2,2) and by the connecting cycle (1,2,1)). Even if the profit made for every pound of fibre depends upon the colour of the fibre, the points, Z_1, Z_2 and Z_3 are still aligned. This implies that only point X or point Y can represent the optimal solution and again the average profit of such a point can be approximated by means of a number of selfloops equal to the number of colours, a rather intuitive result.

REFERENCES

[1]   E.L. Lawler, "Optimal Cycles in Graphs and the Minimal Cost-to-Time Ratio
       Problem" in 'Periodic Optimization' edited by A. Marzollo, CISM —
       Springer Verlag, 1973.

[2]   A. Locatelli, P. Migliarese and S. Rinaldi, "Constrained Periodic Optimiza-
       tion of Finite Automata" in 'Periodic Optimization' edited by A.
       Marzollo, CISM — Springer Verlag 1973.

[3]   E. L. Lawler, and S. Rinaldi, "Optimal Constrained Cycles in Graphs"
       Proceedings of Int. Symp. on Systems Engineering and Analysis,
       Purdue Univ., Lafayette, Oct. 1972.

[4]   G.B. Dantzig, W.O. Blattner and M.R. Rao, "Finding Cycle in a Graph with
       Minimum Cost-to-Time Ratio with Application to a Ship Routing
       Problem" Theory of Graphs, Int. Symp., Roma, Italy, July 1966,
       published by Dunod, Paris and Gordon and Breach, N.Y., pp. 77-83.

[5]   A. Locatelli, P. Migliarese and S. Rinaldi, "Periodic Optimization of Finite
       Automata" IEEE Conference on Systems Engineering and Society,
       Washington, D.C., Oct. 1972.

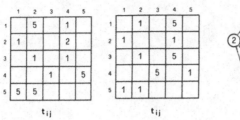

Fig. 3.1

Iteration	C	Cycle	$\Sigma \bar{c}_{ij}(C)$	Σt_{ij}
1	5	(1,2,1)	-4	2
2	3	(1,4,5,1)	-10	7
3	11/7	(1,4,5,2,1)	-4/7	8
4	3/2	(1,4,3,2,1)	-14	12
5	1/3	(1,4,3,4,3,2,1)	-4/3	22
6	3/11	(1,4,3,4,3,2,1)	0	22

Fig. 3.2

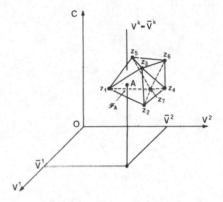

Fig. 5.1

c_{ij}	1	2	3
1	6	1	
2	1	12	9
3	5		2

t_{ij}	1	2	3
1	2	1	
2	1	3	3
3	1		1

v_{ij}	1	2	3
1	2	2	
2	2	6	5
3	8		5

Fig. 6.1

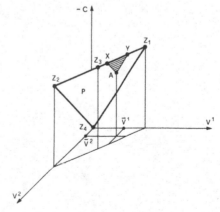

Fig. 7.1

THE TRAVELING SALESMAN PROBLEM AND ITS IMPLICATIONS (*)

F. Maffioli (**)

Abstract

The aim of this review is to outline the main exact and approximate approaches to the traveling salesman problem (TSP), the various problems arisen from recent work on this subject, the particular cases in which an efficient solution method can be implemented and the connections of the TSP with other topics of combinatorial optimization such as matroids and computational complexity.

1. INTRODUCTION

Let $G = (N,A)$ be an undirected arc-weighted graph, $N = \{1, 2, \ldots, n\}$ being the set of nodes and $A = \{(i, j), i \neq j = 1, 2, \ldots, n\}$ being the set of arcs of G. Let a_{ij} be the weight of arc (i, j). A sequence of arcs of the type $(i_1, i_2), (i_2, i_3), \ldots, (i_k, i_{k+1})$ will be called a path if $i_{k+1} \neq i_1$ and a cycle if $i_{k+1} = i_1$. A path (cycle) is simple if it has no repeated nodes (but for $i_{k+1} = i_1$). G is connected if there exists a path between every pair of nodes. If G is directed, i.e., $a_{ij} \neq a_{ji}$, G shall be called a digraph. The number of arcs incident to a node i of G is called the degree $\delta(i)$ of node i. In a digraph we may wish to distinguish between the number of arcs directed into node i, or in-degree $\delta_i(i)$, and the number of arcs leaving node i or out-degree $\delta_o(i)$. A tree is a connected graph with no cycles. A path (cycle) will be called hamiltonian whenever it is simple and it spans all the nodes of G.

The TSP is the problem of finding a least weighted, or shortest,

---

(*) Partially done while the author was Visiting Research Scholar at the University of California at Berkeley, Dept. of Electrical Engineering and Computer Science, under U.S. NESC contract No. N0039-71-C-0255.

(**) Istituto di Elettrotecnica ed Elettronica and Centro di Telecomunicazioni Spaziali of CNR Politecnico di Milano.

hamiltonian cycle (HC). It is well known that this problem is equivalent to that of finding the shortest hamiltonian path (HP) from node 1 to node n + 1 of a companion graph Γ obtained from G with the simple construction depicted in Fig. 1.

The TSP has been approached by many authors, but it is still to be considered unsolved in the sense that no really efficient algorithm for solving it exactly is yet known.

By an efficient algorithm we mean here an algorithm whose computing time is bounded by a polynomial function of the size of the problem (measured by n, the number of nodes of G, in the case of the TSP).

It is also strongly believed /11/ that such an algorithm will never be found and some evidence for this conjecture will be reviewed in the following.

Section 2, 3 and 4 will be devoted to the most recent approaches to the exact solution of the TSP together with the related bounding procedures. Section 5 will review some particular cases for which a polynomial bounded algorithm is known to exist; section 6 will outline some of the existing heuristic methods together with a result on their behaviour for very large n. The last sections will treat the matroid generalization of the TSP and its implications.

2. EXACT SOLUTION OF THE TSP AND HEURISTICALLY GUIDED SEARCH

All the most recent approaches towards solving exactly the TSP /2, 6, 9, 10,22/ use some kind of lower bound to the length of the solution to guide a search of the type known as branch-and-bound /13/ or heuristically guided search (HGS) /8,19/.

The next two sections will consider the problem of finding good lower bounds. By now we need only to assume that such a bound is available, i.e., that we have an efficient algorithm to compute a lower bound. Let C* be the length of a TSP solution and C be a lower bound spanning the same graph G.

Since branch-and-bound methods will be dealt with in some other part of this set of lectures /24/ let us briefly review here the HGS when applied to the TSP /2,6/, viewed as the problem of finding a shortest HP of G between node 1 and n.

Let us construct a digraph D = (V,T) from the given graph G = (N,A) in the following way. Each vertex $v_i \in V$ represents a subset S_i of N and a "last node" n_i.

We say that a link (v_i, v_j) belongs to T iff $S_j = S_i + \{ n_j \}$ and there exists an arc of G connecting n_i to n_j. The weight t_{ij} of link (v_i, v_j) will be equal to the length a_{ij} of arc (n_i, n_j) of G. There will be an initial vertex v_a of D, characterized by $S_a = \{1\}$ and $n_a = 1$, and a final vertex v_z, characterized by $S_z = N$ and $n_z = n$.

Let then d_{ij} be the cost of a minimum path leading from v_i to v_j on D.

For each vertex v_i a parameter p_i is defined and V is partitioned with respect to p_i into three classes.

a) "closed" vertices, for which p_i is known to be equal to $d_{a,i} \triangleq d_i$, the distance of v_i from the initial vertex v_a.

b) "open" vertices, for which $p_i \geqslant d_i$.

c) "blank" vertices, for which p_i is unknown.

Assume also that an estimate q_i of $d_{i,z}$, the distance between v_i and v_z is available from the problem domain, such that

$$q_i \leqslant d_{i,j} + q_j .$$

A general step of the HGS is therefore as follows.

— Choose among the open v_i's one for which $f_i = p_i + q_i$ is minimum and put it among the closed vertices.

— "Expand" v_i, i.e., V v_k such that $(v_i, v_k) \epsilon$ T compute

$$p_k = p_i + t_{i,k} \qquad \text{if} \quad v_k \quad \text{was blank}$$
$$p_k = \min(p_k , p_i + t_{i,k}) \qquad \text{if} \quad v_k \quad \text{was open,}$$

and the corresponding q_k's and f_k's.

— Terminate whenever v_z is closed.

D has been constructed in such a way that, by setting q_i equal to the lower bound to the HP in the subgraph of G induced by the set $N - S_i + \{n_i\}$, p_z will be , once v_z is closed, the cost of the SHP of G. Therefore tracing back the path which has lead us from v_a to v_z will yield the solution of the TSP.

Needless to say these methods have an upper bound on the computing time which is an exponential function of n.

3. LOWER BOUNDS

Several lower bounds to the length of the shortest HC (HP) may be used to guide the search depending on which one of the properties a HC (HP) is relaxed, and in so doing depending on which simpler problem has to be solved to obtain the value of the bound. To clarify this let us define a HC or a HP in several ways, and introduce some other concept as well.

Definition 1. Given a symmetric arc-weighted graph the problem of finding n arcs such that exactly 2 arcs are incident to each of the nodes of N and the sum of their weights is minimum is called assignment (A) problem.

Definition 2. Given an arc-weighted digraph D the problem of finding a shortest spanning tree (SST) of D such that $\exists$ a directed path from node 1 to every other node and that no more than one arc is entering each node is called here the shortest spanning rooted tree (SRT) problem.

Definition 3. a HC is a connected A (assignment).

Definition 4. A HP is a ST such that no node has degree greater than 2.

Definition 5. A HP is a ST such that $\delta_o(j) = 1, \forall j \neq n$ and $\delta_o(n) = 0$.

Fig. 2 shows some examples of the above defined items. Let ℓ_A, ℓ_T, ℓ_R be respectively the lengths of the shortes assignment, of the shortest spanning tree, and of the shortest spanning rooted tree. From definition 3, 4 and 5 it follows that

$$\ell_A \leq \ell_{HC}$$

$$\ell_T \leq \ell_{HP}$$

$$\ell_R \leq \ell_{HP}$$

where ℓ_{HC} and ℓ_{HP} are respectively the lengths of the shortest hamiltonian cycle and of the shortest hamiltonian path.

The assignment problem, the shortest spanning tree problem and the shortest spanning rooted tree problem are all solvable in the sense mentioned in the introduction.

Unfortunately none of the corresponding bound is close enough to direct the search efficiently. The next section will therefore be devoted to methods to improve these bounds.

4. BETTER LOWER BOUNDS

The advantage of having a good lower bound to guide the search is so important in terms of computing time saving that it has been found convenient to develop fairly sophisticated techniques combinatorial or not to get tighter and tighter bounds starting with those mentioned in the previous section.

A combinatorial technique has been suggested by Christofides (1972) /3/ and used in a branch-and-bound approach /22/.

Let the i-th cycle produced by solving the A problem be called $S_{1,i}$ and let n_1 be the number of cycles.

A contraction is defined as the operation of replacing each cycle with a single node, thus forming a new graph of n_1 nodes. The distance matrix D = $d_1(S_{1,j} \, S_{1,i})$ of the contracted graph is taken as

$$d_1(S_{1,j}, S_{1,i}) = \min_{\substack{k_i \,\epsilon\, S_{1,i} \\ k_j \,\epsilon\, S_{1,j}}} \{f_1(k_i, k_j)\}$$

where $F = \{f_1(k_1, k_j)\}$ is the resulting relative distance matrix of the original graph at the end of the solution to the A problem by the Hungarian method.

A compression is defined as the operation of transforming a distance matrix which does not satisfy the triangularity condition into one that does, replacing every distance d_{ij} for which $d_{ij} > d_{ik} + d_{kj}$ for some k by the value $\min_k \{d_{ik} + d_{kj}\}$ until $\forall (i,j)$, $d_{ij} \leq d_{ik} + d_{kj}$ for any k.

The algorithm to calculate the lower bound goes as follows.

Step 1. Set D equal to the distance matrix of the given graph and set L = 0.

Step 2. If D satisfies the triangularity condition go to 3, if not compress D until it does.

Step 3. Solve the Assignment problem. Let ℓ_A be the value of the solution. Set L = = L + ℓ_A.

Step 4. Contract D, replacing cycles by single nodes.

Step. 5. If D is now 1 x 1, go to 6, otherwise return to 2.

Step 6. L is the required lower bound for the TSP.

An example of the application of this algorithm is depicted in Fig. 3.

An extensive testing /3/ has shown that this algorithm produces bound 4 % off the optimum in the average. The computational complexity of the algorithm is of order k n^3, where k is a constant slightly bigger than that resulting from solving the A problem only.

A completely different technique has been discovered by Held and Karp (1971) /9, 10/ and slightly improved in /2/; this method takes as its starting point a well known fact, namely that the difference between the lengths of two HC's is invariant under modifications of the distance matrix of the type

$$a'_{ij} = a_{ij} + \pi_i + \pi_j \quad , \quad \forall \ (i,j)$$

π being a vector of real constants. Let a one-tree be defined as the subgraph of G obtained adjoining to any tree spanning N-{1} the two shortest arcs connected with node 1 and let T_k be a general one-tree.

Let ℓ_k and ℓ_k' be the lengths of T_k respectively under matrix $\{a_{ij}\}$ and $\{a'_{ij}\}$. Then

$$\ell'_k = \ell_k + \sum_{j=1}^{n} \pi_j \delta_{kj}$$

δ_{kj} being the degree of node j in T_k.

Let ℓ_o and ℓ'_o be the lengths of a shortest HC, then

$$\ell'_o = \ell_o + 2 \sum_{j=1}^{n} \pi_j$$

since every node is of degree 2 in a HC. But a HC is a particular one-tree so that

$$\ell'_o \geqslant \min_k \ell'_k$$

from which we have

$$\ell_o \geqslant w(\mu) = \min_k \{\ell_k + \pi \cdot \mu_k\}$$

where x.y denotes the inner product of x and y, and μ_k is a vector such that

$$\mu_{kj} = \delta_{kj} - 2 \quad , \quad \forall \ j.$$

Then also

$$\ell_o \geqslant \max_{\pi} \ w(\pi) = w(\bar{\pi}) \qquad (*)$$

and the best bound will correspond to $\bar{\pi}$.

Unfortunately inequality (*) very seldom holds with an equal sign since a "gap" may be shown to exist between $w(\bar{\pi})$ and ℓ_o in most cases /9/. To find $\bar{\pi}$ an iterative procedure has been implemented /2, 10/.

$$\pi^o = 0$$
$$\pi^{m+1} = \pi^m + t_m s^m$$

where $\{t_m\}$ is a sequence of a scalars and s^m is a suitable direction towards $\bar{\pi}$.

A natural choice for s^m is $\nabla w(\pi^m)$ /10/ or a linear combination of this and the previous search direction s^{m-1} /2/ :

$$s^m = \nabla w(\pi^m) + \beta_m s^{m-1}$$

By a suitable choice of the scalars t_m and β_m very good computational results have been obtained so that graphs with up to 100 nodes have been solved in reasonable computing times by a Univac 1108 /2/.

5. PARTICULAR CASES

There are a few particular instances of the TSP which can be solved by efficient algorithms.

The first example of this kind was found by Gilmore and Gomory /7/ in connection with the problem of sequencing a one state-variable machine. Assume $J_1, J_2, \ldots J_n$ are n items to be heated in a furnace and assume J_i has to be taken from temperature A_i to B_i. Let us order the items so that $B_i \geqslant B_{i-1}$, $\forall$ i.

Processing item j after item i has a cost C_{ij} given by

$$C_{ij} = \int_{B_i}^{A_j} f(x)\, dx \qquad \text{if} \qquad A_j \geqslant B_i$$

$$C_{ij} = \int_{A_i}^{B_i} g(x)\, dx \qquad \text{if} \qquad A_j < B_i$$

where $f(x) + g(x) \geqslant 0$. The problem is to find a ordering of the J_i's which has minimum total cost.

It has been shown in /7/ that this can be obtained by first solving the assignment problem and then connecting the various cycles as in Fig. 4. By suitably choosing the connecting arcs and the order in which the cycles have to be considered, an optimum solution is found.

A second particular case is due to Lawler (1971) /14/ and requires the distance matrix D to be upper triangular, i.e.

$$d_{ij} = 0 \quad \text{for all} \quad i \geqslant j.$$

The assignment problem is solved for a matrix D' obtained deleting column 1 and row n from D. The solution will be in the form of a path P from 1 to n and a certain number of cycles. Backward arcs (of zero cost) are now deleted from all the cycles and other backward arcs are introduced to construct a single hamiltonian cycle. An example is reported in fig. 5. Another particular case which may be shown to reduce to Lawler's is reported in /21/. Quite recently Zadeh and

$$D = \begin{vmatrix} 0 & -1 & 7 & -20 & 3 & -2 & 5 \\ 0 & 0 & 12 & 8 & 16 & 9 & 8 \\ 0 & 0 & 0 & 3 & 7 & 6 & 2 \\ 0 & 0 & 0 & 0 & 4 & 4 & 9 \\ 0 & 0 & 0 & 0 & 0 & -18 & -1 \\ 0 & 0 & 0 & 0 & 0 & 0 & 3 \\ 0 & 0 & 0 & 0 & 0 & 0 & 0 \end{vmatrix}$$

Chuan Chen /23/ have shown how to solve the TSP efficiently when the distance matrix obeys a similarity relation, that is when the following conditions are satisfied for all (i,j):

a. $\qquad\qquad d_{ii} = 1$

b. $\qquad\qquad d_{ij} = d_{ji}$

c. $\qquad\qquad d_{ij} \geqslant \min \{d_{i,z}, d_{j,z}\}, \quad \Psi \, z \neq i,j.$

Finally, since the problem of finding a shortest Eulerian cycle in a graph is solved efficiently, another particular case of the TSP could be that of a line-graph /28/.

6. HEURISTIC METHODS

When the TSP has a very large size, which roughly speaking corresponds to $n > 100$, exact methods become useless because of the enormous amount of computing time they would require. In these cases approximate methods have to be used and to the author's knowledge they may handle problems up to 1000 nodes in a reasonable time. All heuristic methods implement some kind of search for a local optimum starting from a feasible solution or a set of randomly generated feasible solutions. The most successful method was originally conceived by Lin (1965) and has been improved recently /4,25/. This method relys upon the general concept of λ-optimality. A certain feasible solution is said to be λ-optimal if it is not worse than any other feasible solution obtainable from it by exchanging any λ of its arcs with other arcs not contained in the solution. Since the computing time is bounded below by a function of the order of n^{λ}, only very low values of λ may be tried successfully. Lin (1965) has extensively tested an algorithm which chooses the best among a certain number of 3-optimal solutions obtained starting from randomly generated HC's. His results were 4 per cent greater than the optimum on the average. A first improvement as far as computing time was due to Lin and Kernigham (1971), who found a way of reducing the number of sets of λ arcs to be considered as candidate for reducing the length of the solution at hand.

Introducing the concept of multistage 2-optimality Christofides and Eilon (1972) succeeded in obtaining 5-optimal solutions, which have been shown to be only 1 per cent off the optimum on the average /4/.

A completely different heuristic approach has been suggested by Krolak et alii (1971) /12/ who proposed to use man-machine interaction to handle large size TSP. Their method has not been tested sufficiently so that a comparison with other heuristics such as Lin's is not possible.

In general a heuristic method may behave quite badly either because it is not able to find a feasible solution in the amount of time at disposal, or because it reaches an insufficiently good solution. This second case is the only one which is important for the TSP and is called a type 2 catastrophe by Pohl /20/, who has proposed a rather ingenious algorithm based on his generalization of HGS /19/ to avoid or at least reduce the possibility of such poor behaviours of the heuristic. His method is essentially a HGS where

$$f_i = p_i + w_i q_i$$

where
$$w_i = 1 + e - \frac{d_i}{n} e$$

with $0 \leqslant e < 1$, and d_i is the "depth" into the decision tree of the i-th state.

The effect of having w_i decreasing with the depth is to insure a depth-first search iff the added cost decreases within ever tighter bounds. If at some point in the search a type 2 catastrophe occurred, the search would revert to ordinary branch-and-bound behaviour. Another property of this algorithm is to ensure that the approximate solution will be within $1 + e$ of the optimum. Unfortunately the computational experience is still too small to compare this with other heuristics.

The simpler and most naive heuristic is the nearest-neighbour-rule, which in most cases is known to yield very poor approximations. However a quite interesting result has been obtained about this rule /18/. Let the costs C_{ij} of the arcs of the graph be integers and randomly distributed between two integers r_1 and r_2. Let L be the total length of an optimum solution to the TSP and let L_A be the length obtained applying the nearest-neighbour-rule. Then with some weak constraints on the distribution of the C_{ij}'s,

$$P \{L_A / L \leqslant 1 + \epsilon \} \geqslant 1 - \delta \quad \text{as} \quad \epsilon \to 0,$$

$\delta \to 0$ if $n \to \infty$. That is in the limit as n goes to ∞, the ratio between L_A and L tends to 1 in probability.

Similar results would be most welcome for other heuristic as well, but are seemingly very difficult to obtain.

7. MATROIDS AND TSP

Let E be a finite set and F^* a family of subsets I of E. $M = (E, F^*)$ is called a matroid iff the two following axioms are satisfied.

Axiom 1 every subset of a set I of F^* belongs to F^*.

Axiom 2 if I_p and I_{p+1} are two members of F^* with cardinality p and p + 1 respectively then there exists an element $e \in I_{p+1} - I_p$ such that $I_p + \{e\}$ is a member of F^*.

The members of F^* are called the independent sets of the matroid. Matroids are in fact combinatorial structures which abstract the notion of linear independence. A set that is independent in each of two (or more) matroids is called an intersection of those matroids /15/.

As a first example of matroid we may consider the so called graphic matroid. Let $G = (N,A)$ be a given graph and consider the family of forests of G, i.e. the family F^* of subsets I of A such that I contains no cycles. Then $M = (A,F^*)$ is the graphic matroid of G.

Let now $G = (N,A)$ be a digraph.
Let $I_1^{\square}$ be the family of all subsets of A such that no more than one arc is entering any node, and $I_2^{\square}$ the family of subsets of A such that no more than one arc is leaving any node. It can be shown that $M_1 = (A, I_1^{\square})$ and $M_2 = (A, I_2^{\square})$ are also matroids.

Assume now a weighting function

$$w : A \to \mathcal{R}^+$$

is defined. The problem of finding the independent set of maximum weight in a given matroid can be solved by the "greedy" algorithm and is reviewed somewhere else in this text /26/. For instance the problem of finding the SST of G may be viewed as the problem of finding an independent set of maximum weight in the graphic matroid M of G and therefore solved by the greedy algorithm /26/.

Similarly the assignment problem can be viewed as the problem of finding a maximum weight intersection of M_1 and M_2, while the problem of finding a SRT can be viewed as the problem of finding a maximum weight intersection of M and M_1. An efficient algorithm is in fact available for solving any two matroids intersection problem /15/ : the algorithms for solving the AP and for finding the SRT of a graph are particular cases of this algorithm taking advantage of the special structure of the two problems.

It is fairly obvious that a maximum weight intersection of M, M_1 and M_2 would be a longest hamiltonian path, so that an algorithm which would solve efficiently a three matroids intersection problem would also solve the TSP. Unfortunately this algorithm has not yet been found.

A generalization of matroids intersection problems are the so called matroids with parity conditions /16/. Assume a parity is assigned onto the elements of a matroid M, so that for each element e there exists a "mate", $\bar{e}$. It is required to find an independent set I of M of maximum weight subject to the condition that if an element e belongs to I, its mate $\bar{e}$ also belongs to I, otherwise neither one will belong to I. An efficient algorithm has been conceived /16/ for solving this problem, but has been proven not to work in all cases. In any case none yet exists for solving efficiently the more complicate problem of finding I when each element of M has two mates, say $\bar{e}$ and $\bar{\bar{e}}$.

Let us in general refer to k-parity problem as a problem where each element can have k mates. The following theorem is due to Lawler /27/.

Theorem   There exists a polynomial bounded algorithm for the (weighted) 3-matroids intersection problem iff there exists a polynomial bounded algorithm for the (weighted) k-parity problem, for all k $\geqslant$ 3.

Since the class of k-parity problems with k $\geqslant$ 3 is enormously large, we can reasonably conjecture that an efficient algorithm for all these problems will never be found and because of the above mentioned theorem the same is true also for the apparently simpler 3-matroids intersection problem.

This is one piece of evidence that an algorithm, for solving the TSP exactly in a time bounded by a function growing polynomially with n will never be found. Other elements supporting this conjecture may be found in Karp (1972) /11/.

ACKNOWLEDGMENT

It is a pleasure to acknowledge here A. Marzollo and S. Rinaldi for the invitation to give this lecture, E.L. Lawler for the many fruitful discussions, P.M. Camerini and L. Fratta who read the manuscript and made several useful comments.

REFERENCES

[1]   M. Bellmore & G.L. Nemhauser (1968) "The TSP: a survey" Op. Res. 16 pp. 538-558.

[2]   P.M. Camerini, L. Fratta & F. Maffioli "TSP: heuristically guided search and modified gradient techniques" (to appear).

[3]   N. Christofides (1972) "Bounds for the TSP" Op. Res. 20 pp. 1044-1056.

[4]   N. Christofides & S. Eilon (1972) "Algorithms for large-scale TSPs" Op. Res. Quarterly 23 pp. 511-518.

[5]   G.B. Dantzig, D.R. Fulkerson & S.M. Johnson (1954) "Solution of large-scale TSP" Op. Res. 2 pp. 393-410.

[6]   L. Fratta & F. Maffioli (1972) "On the shortest hamiltonian chain of a network" 2nd International Symp. on Network Theory, Herceg Novi (Yu) July 1972.

[7]   P.C. Gilmore & R.E. Gomory (1964) "Sequencing a one-state-variable machine: a solvable case of the TSP" Op. Res. 12 pp. 655-679.

[8]   P.E. Hart, N.L. Nillson & B. Raphael (1968) "A formal basis for the heuristic determination of minimum cost paths" IEEE Trans. on SCC 4 pp. 100-107.

[9]   M. Held & R.M. Karp (1970) "The TSP and minimum spanning trees" Op. Res. 18 pp. 1138-1162.

[10] M. Held & R.M. Karp (1971) "The TSP and minimum spanning trees": part II" Math Programm. 1 pp. 6-25.

[11] R.M. Karp (1972) "Reducibility among combinatorial problems" in Complexity of Computer Computations, Miller & Matcher eds., Plenum Press.

[12] P. Krolak, W. Felts & G. Marble (1971) "A man-machine approach toward solving the TSP" Comm. of ACM 14 pp. 327-334.

[13] E.L. Lawler & D.E. Wood (1966) "branch and Bound methods : a survey" Op. Res. 14 pp. 699-719.

[14] E.L. Lawler (1971) "A solvable case of the TSP" Math. Programm. 1 pp. 267-269.

[15] E.L. Lawler (1971) "Matroids intersection algorithms" ERL Memo M-333 U.C. Berkely.

[16] E.L. Lawler (1971) "Matroids with parity conditions: a new class of combinatorial optimization problems" ERL Memo M-334 U.C. Berkeley.

[17] S. Lin (1965) "Computer solution of the TSP" B.S.T.J. 44 pp. 2245-2269.

[18] V.A. Pevepeliche & E.X. Gimadi (1969) "On the problem of finding the minimal hamiltonian circuit on a graph with weighted arcs" Diskret Analyz. 15 pp. 57-65. In russian.

[19] I. Pohl (1970) "Heuristic search viewed as path finding in a graph" Artificial Intelligence 1 pp. 193-304.

[20] I. Pohl (1973) "The avoidance of (relative) catastrophe heuristic competence genuine dynamic weighting and computational issues in heuristic problem solving" 3rd International Joint Conference on Artificial Intelligence, Stanford University, August 1973.

[21] M.I. Rubinstein (1971) "On the symmetric TSP" Automatika i Telemekhanika 9 pp. 126-133.

[22]   R. Spears & N. Christofides "A branch-and-bound algorithm for the TSP"
       (to appear).

[23]   L. Zadeh and Chuan Chen - private communication.

[24]   J.P. Barthès (1973) "Branching methods" (this text).

[25]   S. Lin & B.W. Kernighan (1971) "A heuristic technique for solving a class of
       combinatorial optimization problems" Princeton Conference on
       System Science 1971.

[26]   E.L. Lawler (1973) "Matroids and greedy algorithm" (this text).

[27]   E.L. Lawler (1972) "Polynomial bounded and (apparently) non polynomial
       bounded matroid computation" Memo No. ERL-M332, Electronics
       Research Laboratory University of California at Berkeley.

[28]   M.M. Syslo (1973) " A new solvable case of the TSP" Math. Programm. 4
       pp. 347-348.

                              Added in Proof

[29]   P.M. Camerini & F.M. Maffioli (1975) "Bounds for 3-matroid inter-
        section problems" Information Processing letters 3 pp.
        81-83.

[30]   K. Helbig Hansen & J. Krarup (1974) "Improvements of the Held-Karp
        algorithm for the symmetric TSP" Math. Programm. 7 pp.
        87-96.

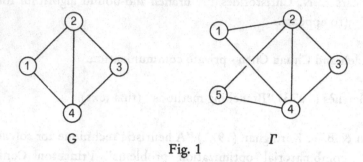

G   Γ

Fig. 1

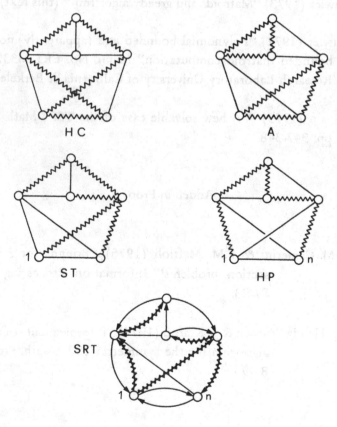

H C   A

S T   H P

SRT

Fig. 2

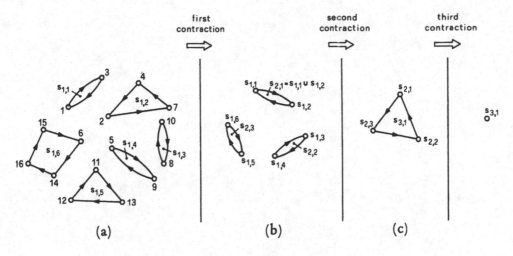

Fig. 3

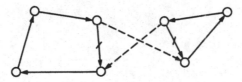

Fig. 4

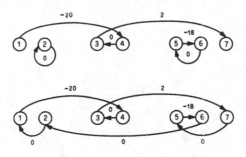

Fig. 5

COMPLEXITY OF COMBINATORIAL COMPUTATIONS (*)

E.L. Lawler (**)

1. THE ISSUE OF COMPLEXITY

It is clear that there is no difficulty in solving virtually any combinatorial optimization problem in principle. None of the questions of insolvability, which are the central focus of recursive function theory, are an issue. If we wish to solve any given problem, all we need to do, in principle, is to make a list of all possible feasible solution, evaluate the cost of each one, and choose the best. This "solves" the problem at hand.

But if we try to apply this approach to, say, the traveling salesman problem, we immediately see that there are some very formidable difficulties. For instance, in a problem with n cities, there are (n-1)! possible tours or feasible solutions. Even if we can list and evaluate these tours at the rate of one per nanosecond, a problem with only, say, n = 30 cities will require many hundreds of thousands of years for solution. No possible technological improvement in the speed of computers will change this situation significantly.

Thus, the central issue of combinatorial optimization is one of computational complexity. We cannot consider a problem to be "solved" unless we are able to specify an algorithm which yields a solution within a "reasonable" period of time.

2. THE NOTION OF POLYNOMIAL BOUNDED COMPUTATIONS

How can we make the notion of "reasonableness" precise ? One commonly accepted notion of "reasonableness", is that of a polynomial-bounded

(*) This work has been supported by the U.S. Air Force Office of Scientific Research Grant 71-2076.
(**) Dept. of Electrical Engineering and Computer Science, University of California at Berkeley, U.S.A.

number of computational steps, as we shall explain.

For every combinatorial optimization problem there is some natural measure of this size of the problem, related to the number of bits of information required to specify the input data for a specific instance of the problem. In the case of the traveling salesman problem, it is appropriate to adopt the number of cities, n, as this measure of size.

For any given algorithm, we imagine its execution on a computer of conventional design, with more-or-less standard instruction codes, but idealized in the sense that the main memory is unrestricted in size, and all questions of input and output are eliminated. If the number of computational steps – in the worst case – is bounded from above by a polynomial function of the size of the problem instance to be solved, we consider the algorithm to be "good" and the combinatorial problem to be "solved".

The reader may question the appropriateness of equating polynomial boundedness with computational efficiency. And there is, of course, good reason to ask why we should prefer an algorithm requiring, say, 10^{20} x n^{100} steps to one requiring $(1.01)^n$ steps. In answer, we can give the following justifications:

(2.1) Machine Independence

The notion of polynomial boundedness is essentially machine independent. That is, an algorithm which is polynomial bounded for one type of computer, e.g. an idealized Univac 1108, will be polynomial bounded when executed on virtually any other computer, e.g. an idealized ILLIAC 4 or a Turing machine

(2.2) Asymptotic Behavior

A polynomial-bounded algorithm requires fewer computational steps than a nonpolynomial bounded one, for all but a finite number of problem instances. (Admittedly, those values of n for which $(1.01)^n < 10^{20}$ x n^{100} may be precisely those of practical interest, but in practice this is unlikely.)

(2.3) Accordance with Experience

Experience tends to indicate that polynomial-bounded algorithms do indeed tend to be preferable to those which are not.

(2.4) Susceptability to Theoretical Analysis

The notion of polynomial boundedness lends itself well to theoretical analysis, as indicated below.

3. COMBINATORIAL PROBLEMS
FORMULATED AS RECOGNITION PROBLEMS

One very good way to proceed with a theoretical analysis of the inherent complexity of combinatorial optimization problems is to view these problems as "recognition" problems for formal languages.

The reader is probably aware that a formal language is nothing more than a set of sentences or strings of symbols drawn from an underlying alphabet. The recognition problem is simply to determine whether or not a given string of symbols is indeed a sentence of the language.

A recognition problem related to the traveling salesman problem can be formulated as follows. Let the matrix of integer arc lengths of the network be encoded as a single string of symbols. (Take the first row of the matrix, follow it by the second, etc., with appropriate punctuation.) Concatenate to this string a number k which is an upper bound on the length of a shortest tour in the network.

Consider the formal language consisting of all strings formed as in the above paragraph. The recognition problem for this language now amounts to the following. Given a string of symbols, interpret (if possible) this string as a matrix of arc lengths and an integer k. Accept this string as a sentence of the language if the network contains a tour of length not greater than k; otherwise reject the string.

4. COOK'S THEOREM

Now consider a very simple and basic recognition problem known as the satisfiability problem. A Boolean expression in conjunctive normal form, or "product of sums" form, e.g. $(A + \bar{B})(\bar{A} + \bar{B})(A + \bar{B} + C)$, is said to be satisfiable if there is some assignement of "true" and "false" values to its variables, such that the expression evaluates to "true". For example, let A = true, B = false, C = true (or false) and the expression above is seen to be satisfiable.

There is no known polynomial bounded algorithm for solving the recognition problem for the formal language consisting of all satisfiable Boolean expressions in conjunctive normal form. That is, no known algorithm requires only a polynomial bounded number of steps when execution is to be performed by a physically realizable computing device. There is, however, such an algorithm, if execution is performed by a physically unrealizable computer known as the nondeterministic Turing machine.

The reader is assumed to be somewhat familiar with the notion of an ordinary (deterministic) Turing machine, with its finite set of symbols, infinite tape, finite — state reading head, etc. A nondeterministic Turing machine is like an ordinary Turing machine, except that state transitions are not necessarily uniquely determined. That is, for any state — symbol combination, a multiplicity of state transitions may be possible.

A nondeterministic Turing machine is said to accept an input tape if there exists some permissible sequence of state transitions leading to an accepting state.

There is no recognition problem which can be solved by a nondeterministic Turing machine that cannot also be solved by a deterministic Turing machine, if the latter is permitted enough time. There are, however, problems which the nondeterministic Turing machine can solve much more efficiently. Roughly speaking, this is because the nondeterministic machine is capable of "guessing" the correct solution, whereas the deterministic machine must, in effect, try all possible solutions to find the correct one. For example, in the case of the satisfiability problem, the nondeterministic Turing machine can guess at a set of values for the Boolean variables and then simply verify that this guess does in fact result in satisfiability.

We make the following two conjectures:

Conjecture 4.1

The satisfieability problem cannot be solved in a polynomial-bounded number of steps by any deterministic Turing machine. (It is known that this is possible for a nondeterministic machine.)

Conjecture 4.2

There are recognition problems which can be solved in a polynomial bounded number of steps by nondeterministic Turing machines which cannot be solved in a polynomial bounded number of steps by any deterministic Turing machine.

We label the above as conjectures because we cannot prove them to be true. However, we do have the following important theorem of Stephen Cook:

Theorem 4.3

Conjectures 4.1 and 4.2 are equivalent, i.e. they are either both true or both false.

The proof of this theorem is beyond the scope of this present paper, and can be found in [2].

5. NP-COMPLETE PROBLEMS AND KARP'S REDUCTIONS

There are many so-called "NP-complete" problems which are equivalent to the satisfiability problem with respect to the notion of polynomial boundedness. That is, if a polynomial-bounded algorithm can be devised for any one of these NP-complete problems, then a polynomial-bounded algorithm exists for each of the other NP-complete problems, including the satisfiability problem, and by Cook's Theorem, Conjecture 4.2 will be false.

The following list was compiled largely by Richard Karp [5], but also partly by Robert Tarjan, by the present author, and by others. In each case, NP-completeness is demonstrated by appropriate problem reductions some of which are quite intricate in nature. An example of such a problem reduction is given in the next section.

Satisfiability Problem – This was discussed above. The specialization of this problem in which each clause (i.e. sum) of the expression contains no more than two letters can, however, be solved in a polynomial-bounded number of steps by the so-called "resolution" technique.

Hamiltonian Cycle Problem – The problem of determining whether or not a given graph contains a Hamiltonian cycle is NP-complete. Moreover, this problem is NP-complete even when the problem is restricted to the class of graphs which are regular and of degree three and, possibly, planar as well. This situation can be contrasted with the very easy problem of determining whether or not a graph contains an Euler tour.

Clique Problem – Given a graph and an integer k, does the graph contain a complete subgraph with k nodes? This NP-complete problem can be contrasted with the following polynomial-bounded problem: Given graph and an integer k, does the graph contain a subgraph with node-connectivity k? A solution to this latter problem has been found by David Matula [7].

3-D Assignment Problem – Given a three-dimensional matrix of 0's and 1's and an integer k, does there exist a selection of k 1's within the matrix no two of which are in a line (row, column or "file")? This NP-complete problem contrasts with the classical (two-dimensional) assignment problem which is certainly polynomial-bounded.

Covering Arcs with Nodes — Let us say that a node "covers" all the arcs incident to it. Given a graph and an integer k, does there exist a selection of k nodes which will cover all the arcs? This NP-complete problem contrasts with the problem of covering nodes with arcs, which can be solved in a polynomial-bounded member of steps by matching theory.

Chromatic Number Problem — Given a graph and an integer k, is it possible to paint the nodes of the graph with k colors, such that no two nodes with the same color are adjacent (connected by an arc)? The author must admit that, at the time this is written, he does not know whether or not the corresponding coloring problem for arcs is NP-complete.

Steiner Network Problem — Given an arc weighted graph, a specified subset of nodes, and an integer k, is it possible to connect together all of the nodes in the specified subset by means of a selection of arcs whose total weight does not exceed k? If the specified subset of nodes contains all the nodes of the graph, we simply have the simple spanning tree problem, which can be solved by the so-called "greedy" algorithm [6].

A Sequencing Problem — Given a set of jobs, each with a known processing time, deadline, and penalty, and an integer k, is it possible to sequence the jobs on a single machine in such a way that the sum of the penalties for the late jobs does not exceed k? If all processing times are equal, or if all penalties are equal, or if all penalties are the same, or if all deadlines are the same, the problems can be solved in a polynomial bounded number of steps.

Feedback Arc Set Problem — Given a strongly connected directed graph and an integer k, is it possible delete k arcs from the graph so as to render it acyclic? This problem is NP-complete, whereas the following problem is polynomial-bounded, as shown by Eswaran and Tarjan [4]: Given an acyclic directed graph and an integer k, is it possible to add k arcs to the graph so as to render it strongly connected?

6. EXAMPLE OF A PROBLEM REDUCTION

As an example of the sort of problem reduction that is employed to compile the list of NP-complete problems in the previous section, we illustrate the reduction of the satisfiability problem to the clique problem.

For a given Boolean expression in conjunctive normal form, we form a graph with one node for each letter in the given expression. This graph is complete, i.e., contains all possible arcs, except that (1) it does not contain an arc between two nodes associated with letters from the same clause and (2) it does not contain an arc between nodes associated with a letter X and its complement $\overline{X}$. We assert (and the reader is invited to prove) that the Boolean expression is satisfiable if and only if the corresponding graph contains a clique with k nodes, where k is the number of clauses in the expression.

An example of this construction is indicated in Figure 6.1. The reader will easily see that the expression is satifieable and that the corresponding graph contains many 3-cliques.

The reduction in the reverse direction, i.e., from the clique problem to the satisfiability problem, can be carried out by the formulation of an appropriate Boolean expression, or by a uniform encoding technique for NP-complete problems devised by Cook [2].

7. CONCLUSIONS

Although we are not yet able to prove it, it seems very unlikely that polynomial-bounded algorithms will ever be found for the NP-complete problems, such as those listed in Section 5. The very size and diversity of the list of these problems seems, of itself, to be strong circumstantial evidence in this direction. However, this is not to say that eminently practical solution methods are not possible, including some algorithms which may be far superior to those known at the present time.

It should also be noted that the nonexistence of polynomial-bounded algorithms does not necessarily imply that the only possible algorithms are those which require an exponentially growing number of steps. There are, of course, many possible growth rates between polynomial and exponential, e.g. $n^{\log n}$. Moreover, the inherent difficulties of the NP-complete problems may actually be quite different.

All of which is to say that we do not know very much at all about the inherent difficulty of combinatorial problems, and that the tools we have available for establishing lower bounds on the complexity of computation are very weak indeed. But that is still another story, beyond the scope of this introduction.

REFERENCES

[1] R.V. Book, "On Languages Accepted in Polynomial Time," SIAM J. Comput., 1 (1972) 281 - 287.

[2] S.A. Cook, "The Complexity of Theorem Proving Procedures," Proc. Third ACM Symposium on Theory of Computing, (1971) 151 - 158.

[3] S.A. Cook, "A Hierarchy of Nondeterministic Time Complexity," Proc. Fourth ACM Symposium on Theory of Computing, (1972) 187 - 192.

[4] K. Eswaran and R. Tarjan, "Minimal Augmentation of Graphs," to appear in SIAM J. Comput.

[5] R.M. Karp "Reducibility among Combinatorial Problems," Proc, IBM Symposium on Complexity of Computer Computations, Plenum Press, N.Y., 1973.

[6] E.L. Lawler, "An Introduction to Matroid Optimization," this volume.

[7] D. Matula, private communication, 1973.

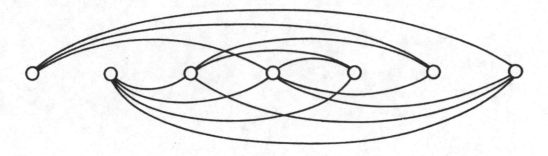

Fig. 6.1

OVERVIEW OF NETWORK FLOW THEORY (*)

E.L. Lawler (**)

1. INTRODUCTION

Our purpose here is to give a brief review of the principal results of network flow theory, including "classical" results and some newer results concerning the complexity of network flow computations.

The reader may be aware that a variety of interesting and important combinatorial problems can be formulated and solved as network flow problems. Some of these combinatorial problems have little, if any, obvious connection with the physical reality of flows in networks. For example, problems in sequencing and scheduling, resource allocation, matching, etc. We shall not attempt to offer applications for the theory described here, but leave it to the reader to consult some of the excellent books on the topic.

2. FLOW NETWORKS

Suppose that each arc (i,j) of a directed graph G has assigned to it a nonnegative number c_{ij} representing its capacity. This capacity can be thought of as representing the maximum amount of some commodity that can "flow" through the arc per unit time in a steady-state situation. Such a flow is permitted only in the indicated direction of the arc, i.e., from i to j.

Consider the problem of finding a maximal flow from a source node s to a sink node t, which can be formulated as follows. Let

$$x_{ij} = \text{the amount of flow throughout arc } (i,j)$$

(*) This work has been supported by the U.S. Air Force Office of Scientific Research Grant 71-2076.
(**) Dept. of Electrical Engineering and Computer Science, University of California at Berkeley, U.S.A.

Then, clearly, we must require

(2.1) $0 \leqslant x_{ij} \leqslant c_{ij}$

A conservation law is observed at each of the nodes other than s or t. That is, what goes out of node i,

$$\sum_j x_{ij} ,$$

must be equal to what comes in,

$$\sum_j x_{ji} ,$$

So we have

(2.2) $\sum_j x_{ji} - \sum_j x_{ij} = \begin{cases} -v & i = s \\ 0 & i \neq s,t \\ v & i = t \end{cases}$

We call any set of numbers $X = (x_{ij})$ which satisfy (2.1) and (2.2) a feasible flow, and v is its value. The problem of finding a flow of maximum value is a linear program in which the objective is to maximize v subject to constraints (2.1) and (2.2).

This optimization problem is solved by successive flow "augmentations" through the discovery of "flow augmenting paths". Let P be an (undirected) path from s to t. An arc (i,j) in P is said to be a forward arc if it is directed from s toward t and backward otherwise. P is said to be a flow augmenting path with respect to a given flow $X = (x_{ij})$ if $x_{ij} < c_{ij}$ for each forward arc (i,j) and $x_{ij} > 0$ for each backward arc.

Consider the network shown in Figure 2.1. The first number beside each arc (i,j) indicates its capacity c_{ij} and the second number indicates its arc flow x_{ij}. It is easily verified that the flow satisfies conditions (2.1) and (2.2), with s = 1 and t = 6, and that the flow has a value of 3. An augmenting path with respect to the existing flow is indicated in Figure 2.2. The flow can be increased by one unit in each forward arc in this path and decreased by one unit in each backward arc. The result is the augmented flow, with a value of 4, shown in Figure 2.3. Note that the conservation law (2.2) is satisfied at each internal node.

An (s,t) cutset is defined by pair (S,T) of complementary subsets of nodes, with s ∈ S and t ∈ T. The capacity of a cutset (S,T) is defined as

$$\sum_{i \in S} \sum_{j \in T} c_{ij} \, ,$$

i.e., the sum of the capacities of all arcs which are directed from S to T.

It is easily shown that the value of any (s,t) - flow cannot exceed the capacity of any (s,t) - cutset. What is perhaps more surprising is that the maximum flow value is equal to the minimum cutset capacity, as stated in the third of three basic theorems, which we now state without proof.

Augmenting Path Theorem

A flow is maximal if and only if it admits no flow augmenting path.

Integral Flow Theorem

If all arc capacities are integers, then there is a maximal flow which is integral.

Max-Flow Min-Cut Theorem

The maximum value of an (s,t) flow is equal to the minimum capacity of an (s,t) cutset.

The Augmenting Path Theorem serves as the basis of the computational procedure described in the next section. The Integral Flow Theorem is the key to the formulation of combinatorial optimization problems as flow problems, and this result together with the Max-Flow Min-Cut Theorem yields interesting results of combinatorial duality (see chapter on duality in combinatorial optimization).

3. MAXIMAL FLOW ALGORITHM

The problem of finding a maximum capacity flow augmentating path is evidently quite similar to the problem of finding a shortest path, or more precisely, a path from s to t in which the minimum arc length is maximum.

Actually, we are satisfied with a computation which does not necessarily compute maximum capacity paths. We propose a procedure in which labels are given to nodes. These labels are of the form (i^+, δ_j) or (i^-, δ_j). A label (i^+, δ_j) indicates that there exists an augmenting path with "capacity" δ_j from the source node s to the node j in question, and that (i,j) is the last arc in this path. A label (i^-, δ_j) indicates that (j,i) is the last arc in the path, i.e., (j,i) will be a backward arc if the path is extended to the sink t.

Initially, only the source node s is labeled, and it is given the special label $(-,\infty)$. Thereafter, additional nodes are labeled, as indicated in the procedure below. When the procedure succeeds in labeling node t, an augmenting path has been found and the value of the flow can be augmented by δ_t. If the procedure concludes without labeling node t, then no augmenting path exists. A minimum capacity cutset (S,T) is constructed by letting S contain all labeled nodes and T contains all unlabeled nodes.

Maximal Flow Algorithm

Step 0 (Start)

Let $X = (x_{ij})$ be any integral feasible flow, possibly the empty flow, i.e., $X = (0)$. Give node s the (unscanned) permanent label $(-, \infty)$.

Step 1 (Labeling and Scanning)

1.1 If all labeled nodes have been scanned, go to Step 3.

1.2 Find a labeled but unscanned node i and scan it as follows: For each arc (i,j), if $x_{ij} < c_{ij}$, and j is unlabeled, give j the label (i^+, δ_j), where $\delta_j = \min\{c_{ij} - x_{ij}, \delta_i\}$. For each arc (j,i), if $x_{ij} > 0$ and j is unlabeled, give j the label (i^-, δ_j), where $\delta_j = \min\{x_{ji}, \delta_i\}$.

1.3 If node t has been labeled, go to Step 2; otherwise go to Step 1.1.

Step 2 (Augmentation)

Starting at node t, use the index labels, i.e., i^+ and i^-, to construct an augmenting path. (The label on node t indicates the second-to-last node in the path, the label on that node indicates the third-to-last node, etc.). Augment the flow by increasing and decreasing the arc flows by δ_t, as indicated by the superscripts on the index labels. Erase all labels except the label on node s, which is now unscanned. Go to Step 1.

Step 3 (Construction of Minimal Cut)

The existing flow is maximal. A cutset (S,T) of minimum capacity is obtained by placing all labeled nodes in S and all unlabeled nodes in T. The computation is completed.

4. COMPLEXITY OF THE MAXIMAL FLOW ALGORITHM

We can estimate the complexity of the computation as follows. Let m be the number of arcs. At most 2m node-inspections, followed by possible node labelings, are required each time an augmenting path is constructed. If all capacities are integers, at most v augmentations are required, where v is the maximal flow value. Thus the algorithm is 0(mv) in complexity.

This result is unsatisfactory in that it depends upon the maximal flow value v. That is, the bound depends upon the very quantity v that the algorithm is designed to compute. We should greatly prefer a bound depending only on the number of nodes and arcs in the network. We would like this bound to be polynomial in m and n, in order to establish the polynomial-bounded character of the computation which the 0(mv) bound does not.

We also wish to establish that the algorithm obtains a maximal flow even when arc capacities are irrational. This is no nontrivial matter, Ford and Fulkerson have devised an example to show that with irrational capacities a nonconvergent sequence of flow augmentations is possible. That is, with a pathologically poor choice of augmenting paths, an infinite sequence of flow augmentations is possible, without converging to the maximum flow value.

We state the following theorem of Edmonds and Karp without proof.

Theorem

If each flow augmentation is made along an augmenting path with a minimum number of arcs, then a maximal flow is obtained after no more that $mn/2$ $\leqslant$ $n^3 - n^2/2$ augmentations, where m is the number of arcs and n is the number of nodes.

The maximal flow algorithm is easily modified to construct augmenting paths with a minimum number of arcs, by modifying Step 1.2 of the algorithm so that nodes are scanned in the same order in which they are labeled. The computation of each augmenting path is $0(m)$. Since by the Edmonds-Karp Theorem $0(mn)$ augmentations are required, the overall computational complexity is $0(m^2 n)$ or $0(n^5)$.

5. MINIMUM COST FLOWS

Suppose in addition to a capacity c_{ij} each arc of the flow network is assigned a cost a_{ij}. The cost of a flow $X = (x_{ij})$ is

$$\sum_{i,j} a_{ij} x_{ij} .$$

We now pose the problem of finding a minimum cost flow for a given flow value v.

Let us define the cost of an augmenting path to be the sum of the costs of forward arcs minus the sum of costs of backward arcs. Thus, the cost of a path is equal to the net change in the cost of flow of one unit of augmentation along the path. An augmenting cycle is a closed augmenting path. The cost of an augmenting cycle is computed in the obvious way, with respect to a given orientation of the cycle, i.e. clockwise or counterclockwise.

Theorem 4.1

A flow of value v is of minimum cost if and only if it admits no flow augmenting cycle with negative cost.

Theorem 4.2 (Busacker and Gowan)

The augmentation by δ of a minimum cost flow of value v along a minimum cost flow augmenting path yields a minimum cost flow of value $v + \delta$.

These theorems suggest an obvious procedure for computing a minimum cost flow of value v. Namely, start with the empty flow and successively augment the flow by augmenting paths of minimum cost, until a flow of value v is obtained.

The computation of minimum-cost flow augmenting paths is essentially a shortest path computation for arcs with positive and negative lengths. Since each such computation is $0(n^3)$ and v augmentations are required, the overall complexity of the computation is $0(n^3v)$. Edmonds and Karp have devised a technique whereby the arc lengths can be made positive, allowing an $0(n^2)$ subroutine to be used to find minimum-cost augmenting paths. This implies an $0(n^2v)$ computation.

6. HUNGARIAN AND OUT-OF-KILTER METHODS

The algorithm described in the previous section is not polynomial--bounded. Yet minimal cost flow problems can be solved by algorithms which are polynomial bounded, in the strict technical sense, as we shall describe.

Some of the best known algorithms for solving network flow problems are based on duality theory of linear programming. These include the "Hungarian" method, so named by Kuhn, and the "out-of-kilter" method of Minty and Fulkerson. These methods proceed by making successive improvements to either the primal or dual solutions to the linear programming problem. We shall not describe these algorithms, but only mention that the out-of-kilter method admits a complexity bound of $0(Cm)$, where C is the sum of the arc capacities.

Edmonds and Karp have devised a "scaling" technique, whereby the out-of-kilter method can be applied to a series of problems, each of which is a better approximation of the given network flow problem to be solved. Each successive approximation requires $0(m^2)$ steps for solution by the out-of-kilter algorithm, and p such approximations are necessary where p is such that $2^p \geqslant \max \{c_{ij}\}$. The resulting complexity of $0(m^2 p)$ yields the desired polynomial bound.

7. LOWER BOUNDS ON ARC FLOWS

An embellishment of the network flow model that aids in the formulation of combinatorial problems is the imposition of lower bounds on arc flows. That is, in addition to a capacity c_{ij} we may designate a lower bound ℓ_{ij} and require $\ell_{ij} \leqslant x_{ij} \leqslant c_{ij}$.

A question which now arises is that of feasibility. Does there exist any feasible flow whatsoever ? Necessary and sufficient conditions are given by a theorem of Hoffman.

In order to state the theorem, we wish the flow network to be in "circulation" form. That is, we demand that the node conservation law (2.2) be satisfied at each and every node. A network with a source s and sink t is easily put in this form by adding a "return" arc (t,s), with $\ell_{ts} = 0$, $c_{ts} = + \infty$.

Theorem (Hoffman)

In a circulation network with lower bounds and capacities a feasible flow exists if and only if

$$\sum_{i \in S, j \in T} \ell_{ij} \leqslant \sum_{i \in T, j \in S} c_{ij}$$

for all cutsets (S,T).

We remark that the out-of-kilter method is particularly well adapted to solving flow problems with lower bounds and that the complexity estimates given in the previous section are valid for such networks.

8. NETWORKS WITH LOSSES AND GAINS

Suppose that flow is not necessarily conserved within arcs. If x_{ij} units of flow go into the head of arc (i,j) then $m_{ij} \, x_{ij}$ units come out at the head, where m_{ij} is a nonnegative flow multiplier associated with the arc. If $0 < m_{ij} < 1$, the arc is lossy and if $1 < m_{ij} < \infty$, the arc is gainy. In a conventional network, of course, $m_{ij} = 1$ for all arcs.

There is a theory for networks with losses and gains analogous to that for conventional networks. Augmenting paths can be defined in an obvious way and "minimal loss" flows can be computed by a procedure similar to that described in Section 5 for minimal-cost flows. However, the Integrality Theorem does not apply to networks with losses and gains and the computational procedures are not polynomial bounded.

9. MULTITERMINAL AND MULTICOMMODITY FLOWS

Many problems require the consideration of networks which admit the flows of a multiplicity of commodities. For some of these problems, the generalization of single-commodity theory is simple and direct. For others, severe complications arise. In this section, we attempt a brief survey of both types of problems.

Generally speaking, there are two ways in which multiple commodities may flow in a network. At any point in time, a network can be dedicated to the flow of one commodity and to the flow of a different commodity at another time. Problems with this character have come to be known as multiterminal flow problems. On the other hand, several commodities may flow in the network simultaneously. Such problems are referred to as multicommodity problems. In engineering terminology, multiterminal problems involve time-sharing of the network and multicommodity problems, space-sharing.

We can also differentiate problems of analysis and problems of synthesis. Up to this point, we have been primarily concerned with problems of analysis, i.e., finding the maximal value of flow for a given network with certain fixed capacities, etc. A typical problem of synthesis is to construct a minimum-cost network in which a given flow value v can be achieved, for a given set of costs on the construction of arcs.

Let us consider some typical problems of analysis and synthesis.

Multiterminal Analysis

For a given network, we may wish to know the maximum value flow between all pairs of nodes, This can, of course, be accomplished by carrying out a separate max-flow computation for each node pair. However, some short-cuts are possible. For example, Gomory and Hu have shown that n-1 max-flow computations, instead of n(n-1)/2, are sufficient for a symmetric n-node network.

The following realizability result has been obtained. For a given network, let v_{ij} = the maximum value of flow from i to j. Then $V = (v_{ij})$ is the flow matrix of the network.

Theorem 9.1 (Gomory and Hy)

A necessary and sufficient condition for there to exist a network with a given symmetric matrix $V = (v_{ij})$ as it its flow matrix is that

$$v_{ij} \geq \min\{v_{ik}, v_{kj}\},$$

for all i,j,k.

Multiterminal Synthesis

Let $R = (r_{ij})$ be a given matrix of flow requirements, and $A = (a_{ij})$ be a given matrix of arc costs. The cost of providing c_{ij} units of capacity in arc (i,j) is $a_{ij} c_{ij}$. What assignment of capacities to arcs provides a minimum-cost network with flow matrix $V \geq R$?

For the special case that R is symmetric and each $a_{ij} = 1$, Gomory and Hu have devised an efficient algorithm. The more general case can be solved by linear programming, but vastly less efficiently.

Multicommodity Analysis

Suppose we wish to induce a flow of one commodity between a specified pair of nodes, a flow of a second commodity between a second pair of nodes, etc. The sum of the flows of all commodities through a given arc must not exceed its capacity. How can we maximize the sum of the commodity flow values ?

Hu has obtained an efficient procedure for the case of two commodities in a symmetric network. More general cases can be solved by linear programming techniques, but much less efficiently.

Multicommodity Synthesis

As in the case of multiterminal synthesis, let R be a matrix of flow requirements and A be a matrix of arc costs. What assignments of capacities to arcs will provide a minimum-cost network which admits multicommodity flows as large as those specified by R ?

This particular problem can be solved quite simply. Compute shortest paths between all pairs of nodes, with respect to arc costs a_{ij}. If P_{st} is a shortest path from s to t, then provide r_{st} units of capacity in each arc $(i,j) \in P_{st}$ for the flow of the commodity from s to t. The total capacity that should be provided for each arc is the sum of the capacities needed for the individual commodities. That is, obtain a superposition of the shortest paths.

Other versions of this problem with bounds on arc capacities, non-linearities of arc costs, etc. are immensely more complicated.

REFERENCES

[1]   L.R. Ford and D.R. Fulkerson, Flows in Networks, Princeton University
           Press, Princeton, N.J., 1962.

[2]   H. Frank and I. Frisch, Communication, Transportation and Flow
           Networks, Addison Wesley, Reading, Mass., 1972

[3]   T.C. Hu, Integer Programming and Network Flows, Addison Wesley,
           Reading, Mass., 1969.

[4]   E.L. Lawler, Combinatorial Optimization, Chapter 4, to be published
           by Holt, Rinehart and Winston, New York, N.Y.

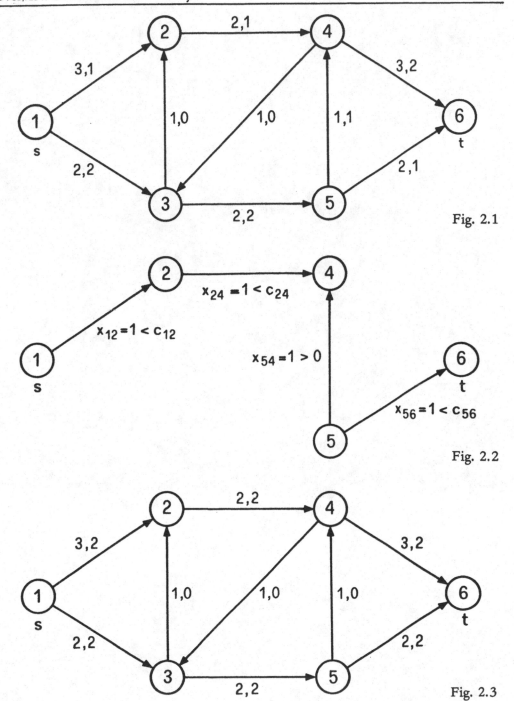

Fig. 2.1

Fig. 2.2

Fig. 2.3

SOME ASPECTS OF DUALITY IN COMBINATORIAL OPTIMIZATION (*)

E. L. Lawler (**)

1. INTRODUCTION

The literature of combinatorial optimization, and of related fields such as graph theory. is replete with numerous examples of duality theorems and their applications: the Max-Flow Min-Cut Theorem, König-Egervary Theorem, Edmond's Odd Set Covering Theorem, Hoffman's Circulation Theorem, Minty's Painting Theorem, Menger's Theorem, Dilworth's Theorem, etc. Our objective in this Chapter is to review a few of these duality results and to give some examples which may be convincing of the usefulness of duality concepts in problem formulation and solution.

2. LINEAR PROGRAMMING DUALITY

There are essentially two types of duality of importance in combinatorial optimization: linear programming and graphic. In this section we summarize the principal results of linear programming duality theory.

For every primal linear program of the form

minimize $\qquad z = cx$

subject to

$$Ax \geqslant b$$
$$x \geqslant 0$$

there is a dual linear program of the form

maximize $\qquad Z = by$

subject to

$$A^T y \leqslant c,$$
$$y \geqslant 0.$$

(*) This work has been supported by the U.S. Air Force Office of Scientific Research Grant 71-2076.
(**) Dept. of Electrical Engineering and Computer Science, University of California at Berkeley, U.S.A.

Linear programming duality theory states that:

(2.1) For all feasible solution x to the primal problem, and all feasible solutions y to the dual problem, $Z \leqslant z$.

(2.2) If either the primal or the dual problem admits a finite optimal solution, then so does the other, and for these optimal solutions $Z = z$.

(2.3) Let x, y be feasible solutions. Necessary and sufficient conditions for x, y to be optimal are that, for all i, j.

$$y_i (Ax)_i = 0,$$
$$x_j (A^T y)_j = 0.$$

The properties (2.1) and (2.2), together with the Integrality Theorem of network flows, manifest themselves as the Max-Flow Min-Cut Theorem. The conditions (2.3), commonly referred to as orthogonality conditions of linear programming, provide the basis for such procedures as the Hungarian and Out-of-Kilter methods of optimization.

3. GRAPHIC DUALITY

A graph is planar if it can be drawn in the plane with no arcs intersecting. A graph has a dual if and only if it is planar. A dual G^D of a planar graph G is obtained as follows. G^D has one node for each face of G, including the face exterior to G. G^D has an arc corresponding to each arc of G, and this arc connects the nodes corresponding to the faces on either side of the arc in G. A typical construction of this type is illustrated in Fig. 3.1. (Note: G^D is not unique because of the nonuniqueness of the planar representation of G.)

The dual of a directed graph can be obtained in much the same way. However, it is necessary to take care to properly orient the directions of the arcs in the dual. One can use a consistent rule such as the following: Rotate each arc in G clockwise until it coincides with the dual arc in G^D. The head of the arc now indicates the position of the head of the arc in the dual. The application of this rule is illustrated in Fig. 3.2.

Some of the principal results of graphic duality are the following:

(3.1) There is a one-one correspondence between the cycles of G and the cocycles of G^D and between the cocylces of G and the cycles of G^D.

(3.2) In the case of directed graphs, there is a one-one correspondence between the directed cycles of G and the directed cocycles of G^D and between the directed cocycles of G and the directed cycles of G^D.

4. VARIATIONS OF DILWORTH's THEOREM

A consequence of linear programming duality, which we shall not prove here is the following theorem (which is to be distinguished from the Max-Flow Min-Cut Theorem).

Theorem 4.1 (Min-Flow Max-Cut Theorem)

Let G be a flow network with lower bounds ℓ_{ij} and capacities c_{ij} for each arc (i,j). If G admits a feasible (s,t) flow, then the minimum value of an (s,t) flow in G is equal to the maximum of

$$\sum_{i \in S, j \in T} \ell_{ij} - \sum_{i \in T, j \in S} c_{ij}$$

over all (s,t) cutsets (S,T).

The Min-Flow Max-Cut Theorem can be employed to prove a classical result of combinatorial theory known as Dilworth's Theorem. This theorem concerns the minimum number of paths in an acyclic directed graph which are sufficient to cover a special subset of arcs. (a set of paths "covers" a set of arcs A if each arc in A is contained in at least one path.)

Theorem 4.2 (Dilworth [2])

Let G be an acyclic directed graph and let A be a subset of its arcs. The minimum number of directed paths required to cover the arcs in A is equal to the maximum number of arcs in A, no two of which are contained in a directed path in G.

Proof:

Add nodes s and t to G, and arcs (s,i), (i,t), for all $i \neq s,t$. For each arc $(i,j) \in A$, set $\ell_{ij} = 1$, $c_{ij} = +\infty$, and for all other arcs set $\ell_{ij} = 0$, $c_{ij} = +\infty$. A minimum value (s,t) flow yelds the minimum number of directed paths required to cover all the arcs in A. (Note that if the graph contained directed cycles, some of the arcs in A could be covered by flow circulating around those cycles.) Apply Theorem 4.1 and the result follows immediately.

We can now apply graphic duality to obtain a new theorem from Dilworth's Theorem. We call a graph (s,t) planar if it remains planar after the addition of an arc between s and t.

Theorem 4.3

If G is an acyclic, (s,t) planar diagram, then the maximum number of arcs in an (s,t) directed path is equal to the minimum number of (s,t) directed cutsets covering all the arcs of G.

Proof:

Let A be the entire set of arcs of G, apply the Dilworth theorem to the dual of G and reinterpret the results in the original graph.

At this point, the reader should be convinced that the joint application of linear programming duality concepts and graphic duality concepts can lead to the generation of a large number of combinatorial duality theorems of various kinds.

5. THE PROVISIONING PROBLEM

We conclude by illustrating how duality theory can be applied to solve what would appear to be a very difficult combinatorial problem. This problem was originally formulated by J. Rhys, and further analysed by Muchland [3] and Balinski [1].

Suppose we are to purchase provisions for an expedition. There are n items to choose from among, where item j costs $c_j > 0$ dollars. Also suppose there are m sets of items, $S_1, S_2, ..., S_m$, which are known to confer spetial benefits. If all of the items in set S_i are chosen, then a benefit of $b_i > 0$ dollars is gained. The sets are arbitrary and need not be related in any particular way, e.g. a given item may be contained in several different sets.

There is no restriction on the number on the number of items that can be purchased. Our objective is simply to maximize net benefit, i.e. total benefit gained minus total cost of items purchased.

Even without any constraints on the selection of items the problem appears to be unreasonably difficult. Yet it can be cast into the mold of a min cut problem and can therefore be solved quite easily.

Let

v_j = 1 if item j is purchased

= 0 otherwise,

u_i = 1 if all the items in set S_i are purchased

= 0 otherwise.

Then the problem is to
maximize

$$z = \sum_i b_i u_i - \sum_j c_j v_j$$

subject to

$$v_j - u_i \geq 0 \qquad\qquad\qquad (5.1)$$

for each pair i, j such that
and

$$u_i, v_j \in \{0,1\}.$$

Because of the 0, 1 restrictions on the variables and the constraints (5.1), it is not possible for a benefit b_i to be earned unless all items j in the set S_i are purchased.

Let us complexify matters by introducing $m + n$ new variables, $w_1, w_2, ..., w_m$ and $z_1, z_2, ..., z_n$.
Consider the problem:
minimize

$$z = \sum_i b_i w_i + \sum_j c_j z_i$$

subject to

$$v_j - u_i \geq 0, \; j \in S_i \qquad\qquad\qquad (5.2)$$

$$u_i + w_i \geq 1, \; i = 1,2,..., m$$

$$-v_j + z_j \geq 0, \quad j = 1,2,..., n$$

$$\qquad\qquad\qquad (5.3)$$

$$u_i, v_j, w_i, z_j \in \{0,1\}.$$

Suppose $\bar{u} = (\bar{u}_i)$, $\bar{v} = (\bar{v}_j)$ is a feasible solution to the original problem. Let $\bar{w} = (1 - \bar{u}_i)$, $\bar{z} = \bar{v}$. Then $\bar{u}, \bar{v}, \bar{w}, \bar{z}$ is a feasible solution to the new problem. Moreover,

$$z = \sum_i b_i \bar{w}_i + \sum_j c_j \bar{z}_j$$

$$= \sum_i b_i (1 - \bar{u}_i) + \sum_j c_j \bar{v}_j$$

$$= \sum_i b_i - Z.$$

Now suppose, $\bar{u}, \bar{v}, \bar{w}, \bar{z}$ is a minimal solution to the new problem. From (5.2) and $b_i > 0$ it follows that $\bar{w}_i = 1 - \bar{u}_i$. From (5.3) and $c_j > 0$ it follows that $\bar{z}_j = \bar{v}_j$. CLearly u, v is a feasible solution to the original problem and again $z = \sum_i b_i - Z$. It follows that a minimal solution to the new problem yields a maximal solution to the original problem.

We need to make a few more changes to put the problem into the form of a min cut problem. We introduce two new variables u_0 and v_{n+1} and mn new variables w_{ij}. Let K be a large number. Consider the problem

minimize

$$z = \sum_i b_i w_i + \sum_j c_j z_j + \sum_{i,j} K w_{ij}$$

subject to

$$v_j - u_i + w_{ij} \geqslant 0, \quad j \in S_i$$

$$u_i - u_0 + w_i \geqslant 0, \quad i = 1, 2, \ldots, m$$

(5.4)

$$v_{n+1} - v_j + z_j \geqslant 0, \quad j = 1, 2, \ldots, n$$

$$u_0 - v_{n+1} \geqslant 1$$

$$u_i, v_j, w_i, z_j, w_{ij} \in \{0, 1\}$$

These changes make no essential difference in the problem. Because u_0 and v_{n+1} are restricted to 0, 1 values, the constraint $u_0 - v_{n+1} \geqslant 1$ can be satisfied if and only if $u_0 = 0$, $v_{n+1} = 1$. If K is a sufficiently large number, all variables w_{ij} are zero in a minimal solution.

Except for the 0, 1 restrictions on the variables, (5.4) is the dual of a maximal flow problem. There is only a superficial difference in the designations of variables and their indices.

But we know that the dual (min cut) problem admits an optimal solution with 0, 1 values for its variables. It follows that we can drop the 0, 1 restrictions from (5.4), retaining only nonnegativity constraints on w_i, z_j, w_{ij}.

The network for the min cut formualtion of the provisioning problem is shown in Figure 5.1.

REFERENCES

[1]   M.L. Balinski, short note, Mgt. Sci. (1971).

[2]   R.P. Dilworth, "A Decomposition Theorem for Partially Ordered Sets",
           Ann. of Math., 51 (1950), 161 - 166.

[3]   J.D. Muchland, unpublished memorandum (1968).

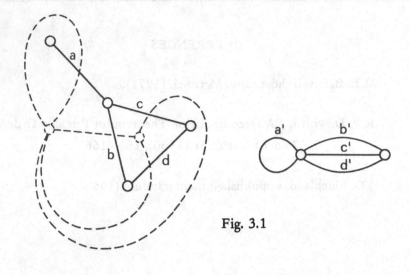

Fig. 3.1

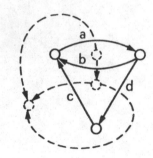
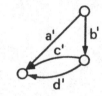

Fig. 3.2

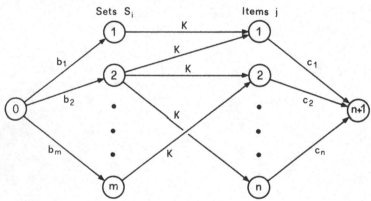

Fig. 5.1

BRANCHING METHODS IN COMBINATORIAL OPTIMIZATION

J.P. Barthès (*)

This chapter introduces a theoretical framework for methods solving combinatorial optimization problems by examining successively subsets of the set of solutions until one of the solutions located in one of the subsets is proved to be optimal, or unitl some user's defined termination conditions are verified. This type of methods includes Branch and Bound and related procedures, Implicit Enumeration and Heuristic Search.

The chapter is divided into three parts: introduction of Branching Methods, Application to the Loading Problem, Application to Pseudo-Boolean Linear Programming.

1. INTRODUCTION TO BRANCHING METHODS

1.1 Combinatorial Optimization Problems

Let us consider a small budgeting problem in the context of a chemical industry. In a chemical plant an important role is played by the Process Engineering Department which is responsible for proposing improvements, for indicating remedies to possible bottlenecks, or ways to increase the quality of the production. A responsibility of the manager of the plant is to find such projects in the limit of his budget in order to increase the overall profitability. To take a concrete example suppose that in such a plant four major improvements have been suggested to the manager by his Process Department.

1 — To install a compressor into one of the refrigeration cycles which does not work up to capacity, at a cost of $ 70,000 for a possible yearly profit of $ 50,000.

2 — To improve the control system on small units at a cost of $ 80,000, yielding $ 40,000.

3 — To increase the heat exchanger capacity to save on cooling water at a cost of $

(*) Dept. de Math. Appl. et d'Informat., Universitè de Technologie de Compiegne, France.

50,000 for a possible yearly return of $ 40,000.

4 — To build new storage facilities to debottleneck the production schedule at a cost of $ 40,000 for a possible return of $ 20,000.

Costs and estimated profits are summarized in Table 1.1. The problem is to find the combination of projects in the limits of the budget ($ 160,000) which maximize the expected profit.

If each project is attributed a variable taking the value 1 if the project is selected and the value 0 otherwise, then the problem may be formulated as follows.

maximize $5x_1 + 4x_2 + 4x_3 + 2x_4$ (1.1)

Subject to

$$7x_1 + 8x_2 + 5x_3 + 4x_4 \leqslant 16 \qquad (1.2)$$

$$x_1, x_2, x_3, x_4 \in B^4 \text{ where } B \equiv \{ 0, 1 \} \qquad (1.3)$$

coefficients being in $ 10^4$.

In this formulation a solution (i.e., a combination of projects) denoted σ is defined as a vector of B^4, the 4 dimensional Boolean space. Such a solution is feasible if constraint (1.2) is verified, unfeasible otherwise. An easy way to form solution classes is to single out a given variable or project.

For example two solution classes may be obtained by using x_1

$$\{\sigma | x_1 = 0\} \text{ and } \{\sigma | x_1 = 1\}.$$

Finally, solving this problem may be stated as achieving the goal of maximizing the expected profit.

Slightly more formally we are interested in problems answering definition 1.1.

Definition 1.1

A combinatorial optimization problem consists of

(i) a set $\Sigma = \{\sigma\}$ of objects called solutions

(ii) a finite set $P = \{P_1, P_2, ..., P_p\}$ of p properties, such that each property P_i partitions Σ into a finite number $q_i(q_i > 1)$ of equivalence classes noted Σ/P_i.

(iii) a goal, G, such that the application of G to a subset of the solution classes $\Sigma/P_1 P_2 ... P_p$ either yields a solution σ_j^* which is an answer to the problem over the particular subset, or indicates in a finite time that such a solution does not exist.

Comments

The solution set Σ may not be bounded.

It could be for example the set of n-dimensional integer-valued vectors. The set of solution classes Σ/P_i is called a quotient set in algebra theory.

Finally since the number of objects of Σ may be infinite, paragraph (iii) of definition 1.1 is a necessary assumption without which convergence may not be insured. Indeed it is easy to prove that the number of solution classes is bounded and at most equal to $(\sum_{i=0}^{p} \prod_{j=0}^{i} q_j)$, with $q_0 = 1$. Thus any procedure for finding the optimal solution by examining irredundantly solution classes is bounded by the total enumeration of the result of applying G to all subclasses. Therefore any such procedure, provided that it does not cycle, terminates in a finite time.

1.2 Graphical Representation

In the small budgeting problem solution classes are obtained for example by assigning a value of 0 or 1 to a given variable (freezing the variable). A possible way of representing graphically the process is to build a graph such as drawn in Fig. 1.1

Such a graph is called a search tree. More generally Fig. 1.2 represents the graph of all solution classes when p partitioning properties are applied. A convenient notation to localize the nodes in the search tree is the following.

The top node standing for the set Σ of all solutions (or objects) is the root; it is said to belong to level 0 and is denoted $S^{(0)}$.

Each node is attributed a superscript indicating its level or equivalently the number of partitioning properties that have been applied, and subscripts determining his position in the search tree. Hence nodes of Σ/P_1, partitioning $S^{(0)}$, are denoted $S_1^{(1)}, S_2^{(1)}, ..., S_{q1}^{(1)}$; and, for example, when P_2 is used to partition $S_3^{(1)}$, the resulting nodes of $\Sigma/P_1 P_2$ are $S_{31}^{(2)}, S_{32}^{(2)}, ..., S_{3q_2}^{(2)}$.

More generally a subset $S_{m_1 \cdots m_i}^{(i)}$ is partitioned into at most q_{i+1} subsets

$$S_{m_1 \cdots m_i m_{i+1}}^{(i+1)} \qquad (1 \leqslant m_{i+1} \leqslant q_{i+1}) \quad \text{such that}$$

$$\bigcup_{k=1}^{q_{i+1}} S_{m_1 \cdots m_{ik}}^{(i+1)} = S_{m_1 \cdots m_i}^{(i)} \qquad (1.4)$$

$$S_{m_1 \cdots m_{ij}}^{(i+1)} \cap S_{m_1 \cdots m_{ik}}^{(i+1)} = \emptyset \quad \text{for} \quad j \neq k \qquad (1.5)$$

$$j, k = 1, ..., q_{i+1}$$

where $\emptyset$ denotes the empty set.

This differs from the definition of a partition in the mathematical sense because of the missing condition

$$(1.6) \qquad\qquad S^{(i+1)}_{m_1 \ldots m_{ij}} \neq \emptyset \qquad j = 1, 2, \ldots, q_{i+1}$$

A path from any node to the root of the tree $S^{(o)}$, is called a branch. Hence the name of Branching Methods given to procedures working with subsets of a set of solutions.

Remark

Although the use of a superscript in addition to the subscript is redundant, this notation is useful in formal proofs. A minimal notation would be $[\, m_1 \, m_2 \ldots m_i \,]$ instead of $S^{(i)}_{m_1 m_2 \ldots m_i}$.

1.3 General Branching Algorithm

The subsets of solution classes being well specified, the next problem is to locate an optimal solution in one of them. The simplest method is to enumerate exhaustively all classes of $\Sigma / P_1 P_2 \ldots P_p$. This method however is very inefficient, since for a twenty 0-1 variable problem ($p = 20$; $q_1 = q_2 = \ldots = q_{20} = 2$) there are 1,048,576 such classes.

Another technique would be to start from the root and to explore successively solution classes all the way down to a terminal node ($i = p$) if possible, to try to obtain a feasible solution rapidly.

Another strategy would consist of computing upper bounds on solution classes, and of exploring areas where nodes have the greatest upper bound (maximization problems).

Although these strategies are different they have some common features. In the general case the strategy may be defined as the answer to three fundamental questions

(i)   what do we do with the node at hand ?

(ii) when do we stop ?

(iii) what is the next solution class to explore ?

The domains of these three questions are called respectively Node Analysis, Termination, and Node Generation.

1.3.1 Node Analysis

In this paragraph we examine a given solution class. First and whenever possible we check the feasibility of a solution class. For example in the budgeting problem, if the frozen variables are such that the corresponding selection of projects is already over the budget value, then it is not necessary to examine the remaining possible combinations of free variables. A lower bound for a given solution class is the total return of the selected projects. For example for $\{\sigma \mid x_1 = 1, x_2 = 0\}$ a lower bound is 5 ($\$ 10^4$).

Second a node status may be defined as follows. If it has been proved that the associated solution class does not contain any feasible solution, or if the node is terminal (i.e. at level p), then the solution class cannot be partitioned again. The node is said to be closed. Otherwise it is pending.

Third if a node is pending then we compute an upper bound by relaxing some of the constraints. In the budgeting problem, we could either ignore constraint (1-2) or replace (1-3) by $0 \leqslant x_i \leqslant 1$ for i = 1,2,3,4.

Ignoring (1-2) yields a crude but easy to compute upper bound, relaxing (1-3) gives the linear programming upper bound.

Finally we define a parameter which is a measure of the desirability for exploring further the branch of the search tree to which the node belongs. The parameter, called the indicator, is the numerical value of a special function called the branching function. A discussion of this function will be found in paragraph 1.3.5.

1.3.2 Termination

We must be able to recognize when we terminate. Termination occurs in three cases.

(i)   Exhaustion. All nodes are closed.

(ii) Bound Test. All the upperbounds on the pending nodes are less than or equal to the lower bound corresponding to the best feasible solution found so far.

(iii) Special rule. Any user's defined heuristic rule.

1.3.3. Node Generation

The step is necessary to indicate the next solution class to be examined, i.e. to tell;

(i)   which is the branching node

(ii) how its solution class is partitioned.

The answer to (i) is the same for all branching algorithms.

Identification Rule

The branching node is the pending node having the highest indicator, i.e. the highest value of the branching function.

The answer to (ii) is slightly more complex. The new solution class to be examined is obtained by applying a partitioning property given by a special rule called the partitioning rule, and among all the produced subclasses the next one to be examined is determined by the priority rule. Both rules are user's defined and depend essentially on the data.

For example in the budgeting problem, partitioning properties consist of freezing variables. The partitioning rule tells which variable to freeze next, and the priority rule says to which value 0 or 1 it must be frozen first.

1.3.4 Algorithm

Step 0

The original problem is examined first.

The whole set of solutions is assigned to the root $S^{(o)}$ of the search tree. At each iteration solution classes are examined as follows.

Step 1 — Node Analysis

1.1 Check feasibility. If it is determined that the solution class does not contain any feasible solution, then close the node and go to step 2; otherwise compute a lower bound if possible and go to 1.2.

1.2 Compute an upper bound for the solution class.

1.3 Compute the indicator by evaluating the branching function.

Step 2 Termination

Determine whether the search has terminated or not by examining the pending nodes of the search tree and by using the termination rule. If yes, then stop; otherwise go to step 3.

Step 3 Node Generation

3.1 Use the indicators of the pending nodes to determine the branching node.

3.2 Use the partitioning rule and the priority rule to determine the new node.

3.3 Close the branching node if all subclasses have been generated.

This is the end of an iteration, go to step 1 for the next iteration.

1.3.5 Branching Function

Let n denote the iteration number, z the upper bound, and g the branching function.

Let us consider the function g(S) which associates to node S the iteration number n at which it is examined. Equivalently let n be the indicator of node S. The growth of the search tree is shown on Fig. 1.3 for the budgeting problem.

With such a branching function one always branches from the last examined node unless it is closed in which case one branches from the most recently produced node that is still pending. An algorithm using such a strategy is called a Branch Search or a depth-first algorithm. Notice that here there is no need for the notion of backtracking.

With the same notations if we now consider the branching function g(S) = -n, then the growth of the corresponding search tree is shown in Fig. 1.4.

The search in this case is done level by level.

It is called a breadth-first search in Artificial Intelligence. It is rarely used in Operations Research.

If we now consider the funtion g(S) = z(S) + 1/(n + 1) where z(S) is the integral upper bound obtained by ignoring constraints (1-2), then we obtain the search strategy shown in Fig. 1.5. This is a Branch and Bound strategy. The term 1/(n+ 1) is used to distinguish between nodes having the same integral upper bounds so that the identification rule may be applied unambiguously.

In the above examples the branching function is defined "dynamically" in terms of the iteration number, n. However, a remarkable feature of this function is that it can be defined in terms of the structure of the search tree, so that it depends solely on the position of the node, on the number of partitioning properties (p), and on the number q_i of equivalence classes that each property P_i induces on Σ. For example let $S \equiv S^{(i)}_{m_1 m_2 \dots m_i}$.

$$g_n(S) \equiv i + \sum_{j=1}^{i} (m_j - 1) \, \frac{q^{p+1-j} - 1}{q - 1} + 1 \qquad (1.7)$$

$$g_t(S) \equiv - \sum_{j=1}^{i} m_j \, q^{i-j} \qquad (1.8)$$

$$g_{BB}(S) \equiv z(S) + \frac{1}{1 + g_n(S)} \qquad (1.9)$$

when

$$q_1 = q_2 = \dots = q = q_p$$

and where $z(S)$ represents an integral upper bound for the problem associated with node $S_{m_1 \dots m_i}^{(i)}$.

It can be shown that g_n determines a Branch Search Strategy, g_t a Breadth First Strategy, and g_{BB} a Branch and Bound Strategy. When those three functions are used the indicator at each node becomes idependent of the number of iterations and consequently of the feasibility of any particular solution class.

2. BRANCHING ALGORITHMS APPLIED
TO THE LOADING PROBLEM

The Loading Problem is a Knapsack Problem (Integer Linear Program with a single constraint) with integer coefficients and Boolean (bivalent) variables.

It can be formulated as

maximize $$\sum_{j=1}^{N} v_j x_j \qquad (2.1)$$

subject to $$\sum_{j=1}^{N} w_j x_j \leqslant b \qquad (2.2)$$

$$v_j, w_j \text{ positive integers for } j = 1,\dots,N \qquad (2.3)$$

$$X \in B^N \qquad (2.4)$$

where B^N is the N-dimensional Boolean Space.

The Loading Problem is one of the simplest combinatorial problems. The small example of budgeting problem (1.1) through (1.3) is a Loading Problem.

First let us examine how the algorithms of combinatorial nature proposed hitherto can be formulated using the General Branching Algorithm framework. The necessary information required by the algorithm in addition to the data (goal or objective function, and constraints) consist of

(i)   a mechanism for checking feasibility
(ii)   a mechanism for computing upper bounds
(iii) a branching function
(iv)   a termination test

(v)   a definition of partitioning properties
(vi) a partitioning rule
(vii) a priority rule.

Once those seven points have been specified everything else follows automatically.

Several algorithms are reviewed now and results are summarized in Table 2.1.

2.1 Exhaustive enumeration

It is interesting to note that exhaustive enumeration can be formulated as a limiting case of a branching method and that very little is needed to bring great improvements.

(i)   Feasibility is verified by checking the constraint setting free variables to 0. This also yields a lower bound.
(ii)   no upper bound is computed
(iii) Branching function is g_n.
(iv)   Termination occurs when all nodes are closed (exhaustion)
(v)   Partitioning properties consist of freezing variables (setting them to an assigned value of 0 or 1).
(vi)   The partitioning rule is the order of variables to be frozen (x_1, x_2, ..., x_N)
(vii) The priority rule says that one freezes the variables to 1 first (for instance).

The corresponding search tree is complete and every terminal node (at level p) is generated. The optimal solution is one of the solutions corresponding to one of the terminal nodes with the highest value of the objective function (there may be several optimal solutions).

The implementation of such an algorithm would not increase significantly the number of operations to be done compared to generating all solutions directly. However this is a very inefficient way to solve the problem.

2.2 Simple Branch Search

If in the previous algorithm we notice that it is not worth partitioning solution classes which do not contain feasible solution, then we obtain a Simple Branch Search algorithm. We only need to add to (i) that nodes are closed when they do not contain any feasible solutions.

The corresponding search tree is shown on Fig. 2.1 for the budgeting problem (1.1) through (1.3), i.e., maximize $\qquad\qquad 5x_1 + 4x_2 + 4x_3 + 2x_4$

subject to $\qquad\qquad 7x_1 + 8x_2 + 5x_3 + 4x_4 \leqslant 16$

$$X \in B^4$$

2.3 Branch and Exclude

The previous method may be improved by using additional information easy to compute during the search. For example once a feasible solution is known, it is unnecessary to examine nodes which would lead to a value of the objective function no better than the one already recorded. To this purpose an upper bound on the objective function is computed. A crude but easy to compute upper bound is obtained by subtracting from the sum of the coefficients in the objective function, the sum of those corresponding to variable frozen to zero. The resulting search tree is shown in Fig. 2.2.

We only need to specify this in paragraph (ii) of the Simple Branch Search algorithm.

2.4 Kolesar Branch and Bound (KBB) algorithm [1]

The next three paragraphs are based upon the same following idea. If the variables of a Loading Problem are permitted to take any real value between 0 and 1, then the problem becomes a Linear Program, the solution of which is an upper bound for any integer restricted problem. The idea is to set certain variables to assigned values 0 or 1, compute the linear programming upper bound for the sub-problem corresponding to the free variables, and to further explore combinations having the largest upper bound. A particular feature of the linear programming solution is that only one variable has a fractional value, all other taking values 0 or 1. We call this variable the critical variable.

Reformulating Kolesar's Branch and Bound in terms of the general Branching Algorithm we have to specify the following points.

(i)   Feasibility is checked by using the constraint; a lower bound may be obtained by setting the critical variable to zero in the linear programming solution of the subproblem associated with the examined node.

(ii)   An upperbound is computed from the solution of the linear programming subproblem defined on the free variables.

(iii) The branching function is g_{BB} (defined in paragraph 1.3.5 of Section 1).

(iv) The termination test is the Bound Test (defined in paragraph 1.3.3 of Section 1).

(v) The partitioning properties still consist of freezing variables to assigned values.

(vi) The partitioning rule is the following. Partitioning Properties (or equivalently here variables) are ordered so that (see eq. (2.3)).

$$v_1/w_1 \geqslant v_2/w_2 \geqslant \ldots \geqslant v_N/w_N.$$

(vii) Priority Rule: variables are frozen to 0 first. The reordered budgeting problem becomes

(E")   maximize $4x''_1 + 5x''_2 + 4x''_3 + 2x''_4$

              subject to $5x''_1 + 7x''_2 + 8x''_3 + 4x''_4 \leqslant 16$

                                  $X \in B^4$

The search tree is shown in Fig. 2.3. It must be noted that nodes of this search tree represents a greater number of operations than nodes of the previous search trees do (Fig. 2.1, 2.2).

2.5 Greenberg and Hegerich Branch and Bound Algorithm [2]

Greenberg and Hegerich improved the algorithm due to Kolesar by changing the partitioning rule, replacing it by

(vi) The partitioning property to be used is that corresponding to the critical variable in the linear programming solution of the problem associated with the branching node.

Results for the budgeting problem are shown in Fig. 2.4.

2.6 Greenberg and Hegerich Branch Search Algorithm [2]

From storage considerations the mentioned authors found more advantageous to replace the branching function g_{BB} by g_n. The search tree corresponding to the budgeting problem is the same as in Fig. 2.4.

2.7 Summary

The previous algorithms are summarized in Table 2.1. The framework of the General Branching Algorithm leads to a standardization of the description of combinatorial algorithms. Also by modifying systematically some of the rules it is possible to define very easily new algorithms and directions of improvement. In particular in the case of the Loading Problem new algorithms can be proposed which bring an improvement of an order of magnitude upon the Greenberg and Hegerich Branch Search procedure.

3. APPLICATION TO PSEUDO-BOOLEAN LINEAR PROGRAMMING

A pseudo-Boolean linear programs is the immediate generalization of a Loading Problem. It is an Integer Linear Program with Boolean variables and can be formulated in the form

$$\text{maximize} \quad c^T X \qquad\qquad\qquad 3.1)$$
$$\text{subject to} \quad P\, X \leqslant Q \qquad\qquad (3.2)$$

where P is an $m \times n$ integer matrix $[a_{ij}]$, Q a column vector $[b_i]$ and

$$c \geqslant 0 \qquad\qquad\qquad (3.3)$$
$$X \in B^N \qquad\qquad\qquad (3.4)$$

As previously, solution classes can be defined by assigning values, 0 or 1, to variables.

A branching algorithm can thus be defined.

A greedy strategy consists of trying to set as many variables as possible to 1 since the coefficients of the objective function are all positive. Some combinations will however violate certain constraints and detecting the unfeasibilities is not so easy as in the case of the Loading Problem. This is essentially due to the unavoidable presence of negative coefficients in the constraints. In order to overcome this difficulty the concept of an "unfeasibility threshold" associated with each constraint is proposed.

Definition 3.1 (see Fig. 3.1)

The unfeasibility threshold for constraint i is

$$IT_i = b_i - \sum_{j=1}^{N} \min \{0, a_{ij}\} \qquad\qquad (3.5)$$

It can be seen that if the value of IT_i is negative (i.e. $b_i < \sum_{j=1}^{N} \min$

{ $0, a_{ij}$ }), then the constraint will never be satisfied. In an algorithm in which variables are set to assigned values, the unfeasibility threshold can be modified by using the following rule.

Rule 3.1

If at iteration $(k+1)$ x_j is set to zero and a_{ij} is negative, or if x_j is set to one and a_{ij} is positive, then the new unfeasibility threshold for constraint i is

$$IT_i^{(k+1)} = IT_i^{(k)} - |a_{ij}| \tag{3.6}$$

Then the value of $IT_i^{(k+1)}$ can be used for a feasibility test. The node generation step of the branching algorithm can then be based upon a slight modification of the concept of cover as used by Granot and Hammer [3]. Take for example the objective function and the first constraint of Balas's example #1 [4], i.e.

$$\text{maximize} \quad 5x_1 + 7x_2 + 10x_3 + 3x_4 + x_5 \tag{3.7}$$
$$\text{subject to} \quad x_1 - 3x_2 + 5x_3 + x_4 - 4x_5 \leqslant - 2 \tag{3.8}$$

By using the concept of unfeasibility threshold it is possible to determine which group of variables, when set to the value 1, constitute a class containing no feasible solution. For instance in (3.8) the classes $\{\sigma | x_1 = x_3 = 1\}$ and $\{\sigma | x_1 = x_3 = x_4 = 1\}$ do not contain feasible solutions. The values of the unfeasibility threshold are respectively -1 and -2. On the other hand setting to 1 variables having negative coefficients in the constraint does not alter the unfeasibility threshold. These variables can thus be overlooked. They only have to be taken into account when for some reason, they are set to 0. Groups of variables such as $\{x_1, x_3\}$ and $\{x_1, x_3, x_4\}$ are called positive covers for the constraint (3.8), or formally

Definition 3.2

A set of variables is called a positive cover denoted K_i for constraint i if

(i) $a_{ij} > 0 \qquad \forall \ x_j \in K_i$

(ii) $\underset{x_j \in K_i}{\Sigma} \ a_{ij} > IT_i$

where IT_i is the unfeasibility threshold for constraint i.

Definition 3.3

A minimal positive cover is a positive cover such that no proper subset of it is a positive cover.

Hence $\{x_1, x_3\}$ is a minimal positive cover, but $\{x_1, x_3, x_4\}$ is not.

In order to obtain a feasible solution it is necessary to set to 0 one of the variables of a minimal positive cover. If in such a cover, K, all the variables are set to 1, then $2^{n-\lceil K \rceil}$ solutions are implicitly enumerated. Therefore by picking the smallest of the minimal positive covers over all the constraints, a maximum number of solutions is eliminated the first time. Such a cover is denoted a minicover.

Definition 3.4

The covering threshold at iteration k, $CT_i^{(k)}$ of constraint i is the sum of the positive coefficients of the unassigned variables.

The parameter is introduced to check more rapidly whether a constraint has a positive cover or not. Rule 3.2 follows immediately.

Rule 3.2

If at iteration $(k+1)$ x_j is set to zero and a_{ij} is positive, then the new covering threshold for constraint i is

$$CT^{(k+1)} = CT^{(k)} - a_{ij}$$

Lemma 3.1

A constraint i has a positive cover if and only if the covering threshold is greater than the unfeasibility threshold. The proof follows immediately from the definitions.

Covering Branch Search Algorithm

(i) Feasibility of the constraint is checked by using the concept of unfeasibility threshold and of covering threshold.

(ii) Upper bound:

$$\sum_{j=1}^{N} c_j - \sum_{j \in I^-} c_j$$

where $I^- = \{ i \mid x_i \text{ is frozen to } 0 \}$.

(iii)   Branching function: g_n

(iv)   Termination: bound test.

(v)   Partitioning Properties: freezing variables

(vi)   Partitioning Rule:

Let $K = \{k_1, k_2, ..., k_p\}$ be the ordered set of indices of minicover for the subproblem corresponding to the branching node $S_{m_1 ... m_i}^{(i)}$, and let I be the set of indices of frozen variables (i.e., $x_i = \xi_i$ for $i \in I$, where $\xi_i = 0$ or 1).

The solution class associated with this node is partitioned into $|K|$ new classes, such that

$$S_{m_1 ... m_i, 1}^{(i+1)} \equiv \{\sigma \,|\, x_i = \xi_i \,, i \in I \,; x_{k_1} = ... = x_{k_{p-1}} = 1 \,; x_{k_p} = 0\}$$

$$\cdots\cdots\cdots$$

$$S_{m_1 ... m_i, |K|-1}^{(i+1)} \equiv \{\sigma \,|\, x_i = \xi_i \,, i \in I \,; x_{k_1} = 1 \,; x_{k_2} = 0\}$$

$$S_{m_1 m_2 ... m_i, |K|}^{(i+1)} \equiv \{\sigma \,|\, x_i = \xi_i \,, i \in I \,; x_{k_1} = 0\}.$$

(vii) Priority rule:

variables of a minicover are ordered such that

$$c_{k_1}/a_{ik_1} \geqslant c_{k_2}/a_{ik_2} \geqslant ... \geqslant c_{k_p}/a_{ik_p}$$

In this fashion, variables with a low average return with respect to the constraint (i) are set to 0 first.

Balas's example # 2

maximize $10x_1 + 7x_2 + x_3 + 12x_4 + 2x_5 + 8x_6 + 3x_7 + x_8 + 5x_9 + 3x_{10}$

subject to

$$-3x_1 + 12x_2 + 8x_3 - x_4 \qquad\qquad\qquad + 7x_9 - 2x_{10} \leqslant 19$$
$$- x_2 + 10x_3 \qquad + 5x_5 - x_6 - 7x_7 - x_8 \qquad\qquad \leqslant 4$$
$$-5x_1 + 3x_2 + x_3 \qquad\qquad\qquad + 2x_8 \qquad - x_{10} \leqslant -1$$
$$5x_1 - 3x_2 - x_3 \qquad\qquad\qquad - 2x_8 \qquad + x_{10} \leqslant 1$$
$$4x_3 + 2x_4 + 5x_6 - x_7 + 9x_8 + 2x_9 \qquad\qquad \leqslant 18$$
$$- 9x_2 \qquad + 12x_4 + 7x_5 - 6x_6 - 2x_8 + 15x_9 + 3x_{10} \leqslant 13$$
$$8x_1 - 5x_2 - 2x_3 + 7x_4 + x_5 \qquad + 5x_7 \quad + 10x_9 \qquad \leqslant 23$$

$$X \in B^{10}$$

Summary of the search

The search tree corresponding to the application of the Covering Branch Search algorithm to the above example is shown on Fig. 3.2. The computations may be followed on Table 3.1.

In the following paragraphs N.A., T. and N.G. stand respectively for Node Analysis, Termination, Node Generation.

Iteration 1 (Column C1)

The original problem is assigned to the node $S^{(o)}$ of the search tree. All variables are free.

N.A.   Feasibility: all infeasibility thresholds (IT) in column C1 are non negative, hence the solution class may contain feasible solutions.

Upper bound (UB): it is computed as the sum of the coefficients of the objective function, since all variables are free. Its values is 52.

Branching function: its value for $S^{(o)}$ is 1.

T.   Test fails: the search does not terminate yet.

N.G.   Branching node is S

Partitioning: the values of the covering and infeasibility thresholds (column C1) shows that there exists positive covers for constraints 1,2,3,5,6,7. The determination of a minicover for the system yields K = $\{x_3, x_5\}$ associated with constraint 2.

The priority rule leads to the ordering x_5, x_3 since

$$c_5/a_{25} = 2/5 \geqslant c_3/a_{23} = 1/10$$

Hence the subclasses of $S^{(o)}$ that will be generated are:

$$C_1 = \{\sigma \,|\, x_5 = 1,\ x_3 = 0\}\ ,\quad C_2 = \{\sigma \,|\, x_5 = 0\}$$

The new generated node is $S_1^{(1)}$ associated with C_1.

The changes in the infeasibility and covering threshold resulting from the setting of x_5 to 1 and then x_3 to 0 are shown respectively in columns C2 and C3 of Table 3.1. The partial solution is recorded in row R1.

The same steps occur at each following iteration. However only the main changes are discussed in the following paragraphs.

Iteration 2

The node to be examined is $S_1^{(1)}$ at level 1.

By looking at column C3 it can immediately be seen that there are still two positive covers for constraints 6 and 7. A minicover is $\{x_4, x_9\}$ corresponding to constraint 6. The updated values of the infeasibility and covering thresholds when x_4 is set to 1 and x_9 is set to 0 are shown in columns C4 and C5 respectively. For constraint 2 the covering threshold is zero at iteration 2 meaning that the constraint will be feasible regardless of the values assigned to the free variables. Therefore it is not necessary to carry out the computations at successive levels. hence the hashed part in Table 3.1.

Iteration 3

An inspection of column C5 shows that no more positive covers exist. Therefore a completion of 1 (setting all unassigned variables to 1) gives a feasible solution (row R2) with an associated value of 47 for the objective function. The corresponding node $S_{11}^{(2)}$ is closed.

Iteration 4

The new solution class to be examined is $\{\sigma \,|\, x_5 = 1; x_3 = x_4 = 0\}$ corresponding to node $S_{12}^{(2)}$. Node $S_1^{(1)}$ is closed. An upperbound of 39 is computed, and without further work this node is closed, since the value of the objective function for the best feasible solution found hithero is 47.

The pending node candidate for partitioning is $S^{(o)}$. The new generated node is $S_2^{(1)}$ at level 1, associated with the solution class $\{\sigma \,|\, x_5 = 0\}$. Node $S^{(0)}$ is closed.

Iteration 5

The new upper bound is 50. The new thresholds are computed according to rules 3.1 and 3.2 and are shown in column C7 of Table 3.1. There exist positive covers for constraints 1,3 and 5. A minicover is $\{x_2, x_3, x_9\}$ for constraint 1. Applying the priority rule yields the ordering x_9, x_2, x_3 and the solution classes

$$C'_1 = \{\sigma \,|\, x_9 = x_2 = 1\,;\, x_3 = 0\} \quad,\quad C'_2 = \{\sigma \,|\, x_9 = 1\,;\, x_2 = 0\}\,,$$
$$C'_3 = \{\sigma \,|\, x_9 = 0\}$$

The new generated node is $S_{21}^{(2)}$ associated with C'_1. As previously computations are shown in columns C8, C9 and C10.

Iteration 6

Node $S_{21}^{(2)}$ is examined. The partial solution is recorded in row R5 of Table 3.1. Column C10 indicates a positive cover for constraint 7. It is found to be x_1, x_4, x_7. Priority rule yields the ordering $\{x_4, x_1, x_7\}$ and the classes

$$C''_1 = \{\sigma \,|\, x_4 = x_1 = 1, x_7 = 0\},\, C''_2 = \{\sigma \,|\, x_4 = 1, x_1 = 0\},\, C''_3 = \{\sigma \,|\, x_4 = 0\}$$

The new generated node is $S_{211}^{(3)}$ associated with C''_1.

Iterations 7,8,9,10,11 (8 and 9 are not shown on Table 3.1).

Nodes $S_{211}^{(3)}$, $S_{212}^{(3)}$, $S_{213}^{(3)}$, $S_{22}^{(2)}$ and $S_{23}^{(2)}$ are successively examined. Upper bounds for these nodes are respectively 46,39,37,43,45. Therefore the nodes are closed and the search terminates.

This example, assumed to be moderately difficult, is solved after a few hundred additions. It is a feature of this procedure to work extremely well on problems having few solutions. For example Balas's test problem #3, having no feasible solution is solved after one iteration.

REFERENCES

[1]   Kolesar, Peter J., "A branch and Bound Algorithm for the Knapsack Problem", Man. Sci., 13, 723 (1967).

[2]   Greenberg, H., and Hegerich, R.L., "A branch Search Algorithm for the Knapsack Problem", Man. Sci., 16, 327 (1970)

[3]   Granot, F., and P. Hammer, "On the Use of Boolean Functions in 0-1 Programming", Opns. Res. Statistics and Economics, Pub. 70, Technion, Haifa, Israel (1970).

[4]   Balas, Egon, "An Additive Algorithm for Solving Linear Programs with 0-1 Variables", Opns. Res., 13, 517 (1965).

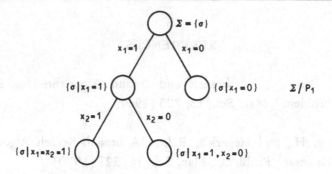

Fig. 1.1.

Partial Search Tree for the budgeting problem

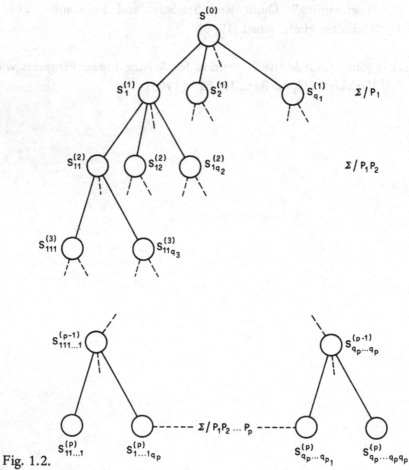

Fig. 1.2.

Search tree representing all solution classes for p partitioning   properties
(dashed lines stand for non represented nodes)

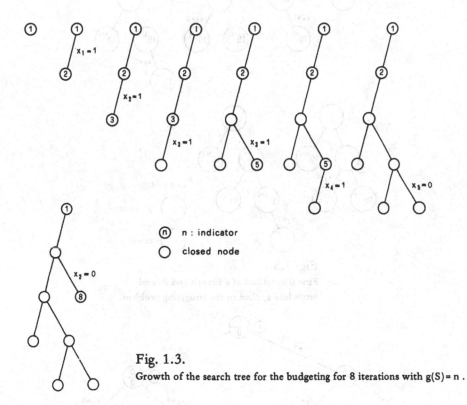

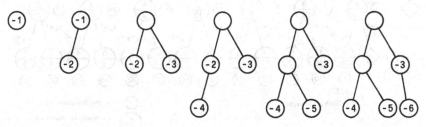

Fig. 1.3.

Growth of the search tree for the budgeting for 8 iterations with g(S) = n .

Fig. 1.4.

Search Tree at the 6 first iteration for a Transversal Search
$(q_1 = q_2 = 2)$.

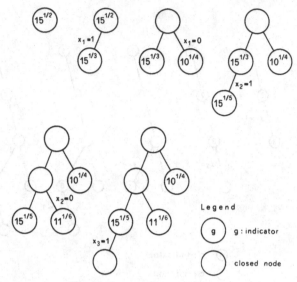

Fig. 1.5.
First 6 iterations of a Branch and Bound
procedure applied to the budgeting problem.

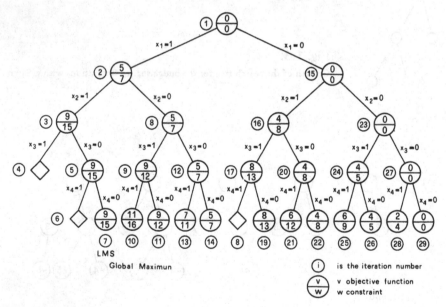

Fig. 2.1.
Search Tree for a Simple Branch Search

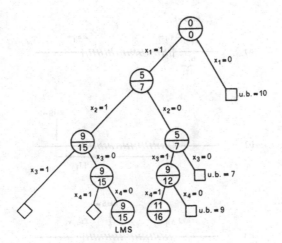

◇   closed infeasible nodes

□   means that no improvement can be obviously obtained by
       following this branch

u.b. is the upper bound at the corresponding node.

Fig. 2.2.

Search Tree for the Branch and Exclude Solution
of the budgeting example.

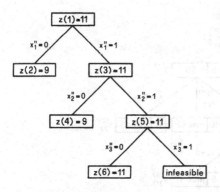

z(n) is the linear programming upper
bound for node n.

Fig. 2.3.

Search Tree for the KBB Solution
of Problem (E'')

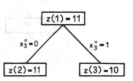

Fig. 2.4.

Search Tree for GHBB
Solution of Problem (E'').

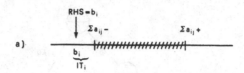

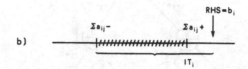

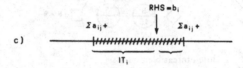

Fig. 3.1.

Graphic Representation of a Constraint

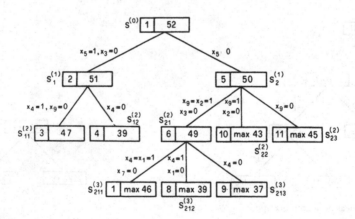

Fig. 3.2.

Search Tree for Balas's Example # 2.

Projects	1 COMPRESSOR	2 CONTROL	3 HEAT EXCHANGER	4 STORAGE
Profit/year ($)	50,000	40,000	40,000	20,000
Cost ($)	70,000	80,000	50,000	40,000

Table 1.1.

Branching Algorithm	Total Enumeration	Simple Enumeration	Branch & Exclude	Kolesar Branch & Bound	G and H Branch & Bound	G and H Branch Search
Node Analysis						
Feasibility Status	Constraint terminal nodes are closed	or infeasible	—	—	—	—
Upper Bound	none	—	compute u.b.	linear prog. u.b. g_{BB}	—	—
Branching function	g_n	—	—	—	—	g_n
Termination	Exhaustion	—	—	Bound Test	—	—
Node Generation						
Part. property	Freeze 1 variable	—	—	—	—	—
Part. rule	Next free one	—	—	—	—	—
Priority rule	to 1 first	—	—	to 0 first	critical variable	—

Legend : u.b.   upper bound

    —   indicates that the rule is the same as in the previous column.

Tableau 2.1.

Various Algorithms for the Loading Problem

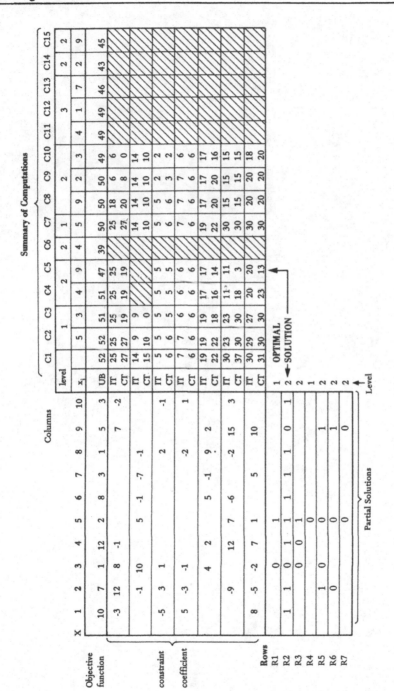

Table 3.1.

Balas's Test Problem # 2 .

ON THE FOUNDATIONS
OF DYNAMIC PROGRAMMING

A. Martelli (*) and U. Montanari (*)

1. INTRODUCTION

Dynamic programming is a technique for solving optimization problems introduced by Bellman [1]. This technique represents a problem as a process evolving from state to state through successive decisions. The problem then becomes one of finding an optimal policy, i.e. an optimal sequence of decisions, which can be obtained by solving a functional equation.

Let us consider, for example, the graph in Fig. 1. and let us assume that a cost is attached to every edge of the graph. We want to find a minimal-cost path between vertex A and vertex D, where the cost of a path is defined as the sum of the costs of the edges which belong to the path. We can say that this graph represents a multistage process. Every vertex represents a state and vertices B_i and C_i belong to a stage of the process.

The number of paths between A and D, among which we have to find one of minimal cost, is $2^3 = 8$. In general, if we have a multistage process with n stages and m states at every stage, the number of paths is m^n. Thus, if we try to determine a minimal-cost path by computing the cost of every path, the number of required operations (sums and comparisons) will be exponential. This number can be greatly reduced by using a dynamic programming technique.

Let us first compute the cost f of an optimal path between vertex A and vertices B_1 and C_1. Of course we have

$$f(B_1) = c(A,B_1) \text{ and } f(C_1) = c(A,C_1)$$

where $c(A,B_1)$ and $c(A,C_1)$ are the costs associated with the edges (A,B_1) and

(*) Istituto di Elaborazione dell'Informazione del C.N.R. — Via S. Maria, 46, Pisa.

(A,C_1). Now, we can compute the cost of an optimal path between A and B_2 and between A and C_2. We have

$$f(B_2) = \min (f(B_1) + c(B_1,B_2), f(C_1) + c(C_1,B_2))$$

$$f(C_2) = \min (f(B_1) + c(B_1,C_2), f(C_1) + c(C_1,C_2))$$

By solving the problem stage by stage, we finally obtain f(D). In general, the solution of a stage requires m^2 steps and the total number of steps is $m^2 (n-1)$, whereas, as seen before, the number of steps required by the brute-force method is exponential.

By considering the graph in Fig. 1. as an example of a multistage process, every edge can be called a decision, that is a choice among a certain number of possible actions. A path can be called a policy, that is a sequence of decisions from an initial state to a final state, and an optimal policy is one which optimizes a given objective function. The formulation and the solution of multistage decision problems are based on the so called principle of optimality [1]:

An optimal policy is one where, whatever the initial state of the process and the initial decision, the remaining decisions must constitute an optimal policy with regard to the new state of the process resulting from the first decision.

The principle of optimality is not stated in a form amenable to precise mathematical treatment and many attempts have been made to put the theory on a more rigorous basis [2-4]. In particular, Karp and Held [5] have given a model of discrete deterministic dynamic programming, which will be presented in the next section, by making use of automata theory. This development provides a theory which can be used in the construction of dynamic programming algorithms or for the proof of their non-existence.

2. THE KARP AND HELD MODEL OF DYNAMIC PROGRAMMING

The formalization of dynamic programming proposed by Karp and Held [5] is based on two central concepts: discrete decision process and sequential decision process. The first concept is introduced to provide a formal definition of an optimization problem. A sequential decision process is more highly structured; such a process evolves by means of transitions and incremental cost accumulation in response to decisions. If a sequential decision process has a certain monotonicity property, then a system of recurrence relations can be given whose solution determines the minimal-cost policies and which can be considered as a formalization of the principle of optimality.

Since the model is based on automata theory, we give some definitions which will be used in this section. For further details see, for example, [6]. A finite automaton is a quintuple (A,Q,q_0,F,λ), where A, the input alphabet, is a finite nonempty set of input symbols; Q is a finite nonempty set of states; $q_0 \epsilon Q$ is the initial state; $F \subseteq Q$ is the set of final states, and λ, the transition function, is a function from Q x A into Q. The automaton starts in the initial state q_0 and receives a sequence of input symbols. For every symbol it executes a transition from state to state according to the transition function λ.

Let A* denote the set of all finite sequences of input symbols. The elements of A* are called words and the empty word is denoted by e, where $e \notin A$. the domain of the transition function λ may be extended to Q x A* by the following recursive definition

$$\lambda\ (q,e)\ =\ q\quad \text{for all}\quad q\ \epsilon\ Q,$$

$$\lambda(q,xa)\ =\ \lambda(\lambda(q,x),a)\quad \text{for all}\quad q\ \epsilon\ Q,\ x\ \epsilon\ A^*\ \text{and}\ a\ \epsilon\ A.$$

Thus $\lambda\ (q,x)$ is the state that is reached if the input sequence x is applied, starting in state q.

The word x is said to be accepted by the automaton if and only if $\lambda\ (q_0,x)\ \epsilon\ F$ and the automaton is said to define the set $\{\ x\ |\lambda(q_0,x)\ \epsilon\ F\}$. A set B $\subseteq A^*$ is regular if there exists a finite automaton that defines it.

In order to provide a formal definition of an optimization problem, Karp and Held define a discrete decision process as a quadruple D $= (A,S,P,f)$, where

A   is a finite alphabet (corresponding to the primitive decisions associated with the process);

S   is a subset of A* (the set of policies for the process);

P   is an arbitrary set (the set of data specifications for the process);

f   is a function (the objective function of the process) from S x P to R, where R denotes the real numbers.

The minimization problem for D is the following: construct an algorithm which, given any $p \epsilon P$, minimizes $f(x,p)$ over all $x \epsilon S$.

To explain the meaning of a discrete decision process, we introduce as an example the problem of finding the shortest path in a graph. The problem is specified by giving a complete graph with n vertices and, for each edge (i,j), a positive real number c_{ij} called the length of the edge. It is required to find a path of minimal total length from vertex 1 to vertex n.

This problem can be interpreted as a discrete decision process as follows. Let $A = \{ a_1,...,a_n \}$ where a_j has the interpretation "go from the present vertex to vertex j". S consists of all sequences of elements of A ending with a_n and every sequence corresponds to a path from vertex 1 to vertex n. P is the set of all n x n real positive matrices (c_{kl}), i.e. every element of P is a possible assignment of lengths to the edges. f is the function which assigns a cost to every path, i.e. if $x = a_{i_1} a_{i_2} ...a_{i_r} a_n$ is a path and if (c_{kl}) is an assignment of lengths, we have $f(x,(c_{kl})) = c_{1,i_1} + c_{i_1,i_2} + ... + c_{i_r,n}$. The minimization problem is now the following: given (c_{kl}) minimize $f(x,(c_{kl}))$ over all $x \in S$.

Now, we can introduce the basic concept, that is the sequential decision process. A sequential decision process is specified as follows:

a finite automaton (A,Q,q_0,F,λ)

a set P

a function $h: R \times Q \times A \times P \rightarrow R$

a function $k: P \rightarrow R$

The real-valued functions h and k are used to add the notion of "cost" to a finite automaton. For a given data specification $p \in P$, $k(p)$ gives the cost of the null sequence e. The quantity $h(r,q,a,p)$ gives the cost of reaching the state $\lambda (q,a)$ by an input sequence that reaches q at cost r $(r \in R)$ and is then extended by the input a. The function h can be extended to the case where we have an input sequence $x \in A^*$ instead of a symbol $a \in A$. For convenience, we may define a function $g(x,p)$ as

$$g(x,p) = h(k(p), q_0,x,p).$$

This function gives the cost of starting in the initial state at cost $k(p)$ and then applying the input sequence x.

The minimization problem for a sequential decision process is as follows: construct an algorithm which, given any $p \in P$, minimizes $g(x,p)$ over the set of all words x accepted by the automaton.

Let us now interpret the shortest-path problem as a sequential decision process. $A = \{a_1, ..., a_n\}$ has the same interpretation as above. The automaton has n states $Q = \{q_1, ..., q_n\}$; the initial state is q_1; the final state is q_n: $F = \{ q_n \}$; the transition function λ is defined as $\lambda (q_i,a_j) = q_j$, for all i and j. P is, again, the set of all positive n x n real matrices (c_{kl}). $h(r,q_i,a_j, (c_{kl})) = r + c_{ij}$ and the initial cost is zero: $k(p) = 0$ for all $p \in P$. Note that every state of the automaton can be put in one to one correspondence with a vertex of the graph and the meaning of $h(r, q_i, a_j, (c_{kl}))$ is that, if we have reached the i-th vertex with a path of length r and we move to vertex j, then the length of the new path will be $r + c_{ij}$. It can be easily seen that the set of all words accepted by the automaton is exactly the set S of paths from vertex 1 to vertex n. Finally, if x is a word accepted by the automaton, then the cost of reaching the final state is

$$g(x, (c_{kl})) = f(x, (c_{kl}))$$

and we have the same optimization problem we had in the case of a discrete decision process.

Although the optimization problem is the same, there is an important difference between the two interpretations of the shortest-path problem as a discrete decision process and as a sequential decision process. In the former case, the cost is defined only for a whole path, whereas in the latter, the cost of a path can be obtained step by step by adding the length of an edge every time a path is expanded by a new edge.

The representation of an optimization problem as a process evolving from state to state through successive decisions is an important property of dynamic programming. Another property which has been recognized fundamental for dynamic programming is monotonicity and therefore we introduce a class of sequential decision processes with a certain monotonicity property. For these processes the minimization problem can be reduced to the solution of a system of recurrence equations of the type normally associated with dynamic programming.

A sequential decision process is said to be monotone if, for all $(q, a, p) \in Q \times A \times P$, the following holds

$$r_1 \leqslant r_2 \quad \text{implies} \quad h(r_1, q, a, p) \leqslant h(r_2, q, a, p)$$

The definition of monotonicity may be extended to the domain $Q \times A^* \times P$.

Now, for $q \in Q$, let $G(q, p)$ be the minimal cost of reaching state q from the initial state. Karp and Held have proved [5] that for a monotone sequential decision process, the following equations hold

$$G(q_o, p) = \min [g(e, p), \min_{\{(q', a) | \lambda(q', a) = q_o\}} (h(G(q', p), q', a, p))]$$

$$G(q,p) = \min_{\{(q',a)\,|\,\lambda(q',a)=q\}} [h(G(q',p),q',a,p)] \text{ for } q \neq q_0$$

(2.1)

Equations (2.1) can be considered as a formalization of the functional equations of dynamic programming.

Since the sequential decision process representing the shortest-path problem is monotone, we can write equations (2.1) as

$$G(q_1,(c_{kl})) = \min [0, \min_i (G(q_i,(c_{kl})) + c_{i_1})]$$

$$G(q_j,(c_{kl})) = \min_i [G(q_i,(c_{kl})) + c_{ij}] \qquad j \neq 1$$

which can be simplified as

$$G(q_1,(c_{kl})) = 0$$

$$G(q_j,(c_{kl})) = \min_i [G(q_i,(c_{kl})) + c_{ij}] \qquad j \neq 1$$

Karp and Held [5] used this model of dynamic programming for dealing with the representation problem, that is for detecting, in an algorithmic way, if a given optimization problem can be represented as a monotone sequential decision process. The main result of their paper is contained in a theorem which gives necessary and sufficient conditions for a discrete decision process to be represented by a monotone sequential decision process. These conditions are given in terms of a property of automata and will not be given here. In [5] several examples of optimization problems are given, for which it is possible to construct dynamic programming algorithms using the above mentioned theorem.

The model of Karp and Held has been extensively studied by Ibaraki [7]. He defines six classes of decision processes: sdp (sequential decision processes), msdp (monotone sdp), smsdp (strictly monotone sdp), pmsdp (positively monotone sdp), ap (additive processes), and lmsdp (loop-free msdp) and for each class of decision processes he gives representation theorems. Moreover, Ibaraki has examined the problem of obtaining an algoritm for calculating an optimal solution for the given classes [8]. Under certain assumptions, he has shown that there is no algorithm to calculate an optimal solution for arbitrarily given sdp and msdp; but such an algorithm exists for an arbitrarily given smsdp, pmsdp, ap and lmsdp.

3. A MODEL OF PROBLEM REDUCTION

In this section we will suspend for a while our discussion on dynamic programming for introducing a formalization of the mechanism of problem reduction. This model will constitute a convenient framework for a more general definition of dynamic programming.

Problem reduction is a well known technique of problem solving in artificial intelligence [9]. It consists of reducing the solution of a given problem to the simultaneous solution of a set of (hopefully, simpler) subproblems. Usually, there is more than one possible reduction, and therefore a decision must be made. Problem reduction goes on as long as all subproblems have been reduced to elementary problems whose solution is known.

In our model, we will make the important assumption that every possible reduction will map a problem into a single subproblem. For a reason that will become clear later, such a case will be called the monadic case. As a consequence, the story of all reductions applied in order to solve a problem will be string-like instead of tree-like.

The second, quite reasonable assumption is that the number of problems under consideration is finite. Problems, however, are not hierarchically organized, so that a chain of reductions may return to the original problem. An obvious model satisfying the above two assumptions is a finite, directed graph G with t terminal and n nonterminal vertices. An arc from a nonterminal vertex V_1 to a (possibly terminal) vertex V_2 means that problem P_1 can be reduced to problem P_2 (we will write : $P_1 \rightarrow P_2$). A terminal vertex corresponds to a solved problem and thus has no outgoing arcs. Obviously, a problem P_1 is solvable iff there exists a path in G (corresponding to a reduction chain) from P to some terminal vertex. In the example in Fig. 2, for instance, problem P_1 is solvable, since there exists in G the path $V_1 V_3 V_2 V_4$ and P_4 is a terminal node.

For our purposes, it is necessary to give some internal structure to problems. We will assume that a problem may have many solutions, each of which is characterized by its cost, that is a real number (*). In particular, a solved problem P_r $(r = n + 1,...,n + t)$ has one and only one solution of given cost c_r. To every arc from V_i to V_j we attach a monadic function $f_k: R \to R$ taken from a given set $F = \{f_1,...f_m\}$ which has the following meaning: If problem P_j has a solution of cost x, then problem P_i has a solution of cost $f_k(x)$. Finally, our problems $P_i......P_n$ have the smallest sets of solutions (if any (**)) which satisfy the above conditions.

   The above definitions can be written more precisely as follows. Let S_i be a set of real numbers consisting of exactly all the solutions of problem P_i, $i = 1,....,n$. If there exists an arc from V_i to V_j with function f_k, we have

(3.1) $$S_i \supseteq f_k (S_j)$$

where $f_k(S_j)$ is the image of S_j through function f_k. Here the $\supseteq$ sign takes care of the fact that for problem P_i other reductions may be possible.

   Instead of writing as many conditions of type (3.1) as arcs, we can derive a more compact relation by making the union of all conditions with the same left member:

(3.2) $$S_i \supseteq \bigcup_{j=1}^{n} f_{ij} (S_j) \cup C_i \qquad i = 1,...,n$$

Here sets C_i are defined as follows

(3.3) $$C_i = \bigcup_{r=n+1}^{n+t} f_{ir} (\{c_r\}) \qquad i = 1,...,n$$

while functions f_{hk} $(h = 1,...,n; k = 1,...,n + t)$ belong to $F \cup \{\phi\}(***)$. For example, for the graph in Fig. 2 we can write the following system:

$$S_1 \supseteq \qquad f_1 (S_2) \cup f_4 (S_3)$$

$$S_2 \supseteq f_2 (S_1) \cup f_3 (S_2) \qquad\qquad \cup C_2$$

$$S_3 \supseteq \qquad f_1 (S_2) \qquad\qquad\qquad \cup C_3$$

(*) Two solutions with the same cost will be indistinguishable in our model.

(**) In fact, the set of all sets of solutions could have no (global, unique) minimum.

(***) Here $\phi: 2^k \to 2^k$ is a set function that always produces an empty set. We put $f_{ij} = \phi$ when no arc is present from V_i to V_j.

where

$$C_2 = f_4(\{c_4\}) \cup f_5(\{c_5\})$$

$$C_3 = f_2(\{c_5\}) \cup f_1(\{c_6\})$$

Note that in (3.3) sets C_i are always finite sets of real numbers, possibly empty.

In order to use system (3.2) for computing our sets of solutions, we need to recall a few results from lattice theory (see [10], for example). Let L be a complete lattice (*) and let F: $L \to L$ be a function. Function F is called monotone if whenever $x_1 \leqslant x_2$ in L, then also $F(x_1) \leqslant F(x_2)$, i.e. F preserves the partial ordering $\leqslant$. A monotone function F is also continuous iff whenever $x_0 \leqslant x_1 \quad ...$ then

$$F(\bigcup_{i=0}^{\infty} x_i) = \bigcup_{i=0}^{\infty} F(x_i)$$

Let us consider the equation

$$x \geqslant F(x) \tag{3.4}$$

where F is a monotone function and let $\bar{x}$ be the glb of all solutions of (3.4):

$$\bar{x} = \cap \{x \mid x \geqslant F(x)\}$$

We can now state the following important theorem [11].

Fixpoint theorem

The greatest lower bound $\bar{x}$ of all solutions of (3.4) is a solution of (3.4), with equal sign:

$$\bar{x} = F(\bar{x})$$

As a consequence of this theorem, we can call $\bar{x}$ the minimal fixpoint of F. Moreover, if F is continuous, $\bar{x}$ can be expressed as follows:

$$\bar{x} = \bigcup_{i=0}^{\infty} F^i(\perp) \tag{3.5}$$

(*) A lattice is called complete iff given any set S (finite or infinite) of elements of L, there exist two elements of L which are the greatest lower bound and the least upper bound of S. For example, the set of real numbers is a non-complete lattice, since there exists no glb of the set of all numbers.

where $\perp$ is the bottom element of the complete lattice L:

$$\perp = \bigcap_{x \in L} x$$

Equation (3.5) gives an iterative algorithm for computing the minimal fixpoint.

Algorithm ITER

Step 1 Let $x^0 = \perp$; $k = 1$

Step 2 Let $x^k = F(x^{k-1})$

Step 3 If $x^k = x^{k-1}$ then stop: $x^k = \bar{x}$ is the minimal fixpoint of F; else let $k = k + 1$ and go to step 2.

If algorithm ITER terminates then it gives $\bar{x}$, otherwise it gives an infinite chain $x_0 \leqslant x_1 \leqslant \dots$ of closer and closer approximations (from below) of $\bar{x}$.

Let us now apply the above concepts to our system (3.2). We can define the complete lattice L_1 of n-tuples of sets of real numbers:

$$L_1 = (2^R)^n$$

The partial ordering in 2^R is simply set inclusion, and the bottom element is the empty set. Extension to n-tuples is done by defining $x' \leqslant x''(x',x'' \epsilon L_1)$ iff relation $\leqslant$ holds for all pairs of components of x' and x''.

System (3.2) can be written as

$$x \supseteq F(x)$$

where function $F: L_1 \rightarrow L_1$ is defined as follows:

$$F_i(x) = \bigcup_{j=1}^{n} f_{ij}(x_j) \cup C_i \qquad i = 1, \dots, n$$

It is possible to prove [12] (but we will not show it here) that lattice L_1 is complete and that function F is continuous. Therefore we can apply the fixpoint theorem. As a consequence, we can be sure that minimal sets of solutions always exist, and that they can be actually computed by algorithm ITER. For instance, in the example of Fig. 3 we have

$$F_1(x_1, x_2) = f_1(x_2)$$

$$F_2(x_1, x_2) = f_2(x_1) \cup C_2$$

$$C_2 = f_3(\{c_3\})$$

Applying algorithm ITER we get:

$$x_1^0 = \phi \qquad x_2^0 = \phi$$

$$x_1^1 = \phi \qquad x_2^1 = C_2$$

$$x_1^2 = f_1(C_2) \qquad x_2^2 = C_2$$

$$x_1^3 = f_1(C_2) \qquad x_2^3 = C_2 \cup f_2(f_1(C_2))$$

.
.
.

Passing to the limit, we obtain

$$\bar{x}_1 = f_1(C_2) \cup f_1(f_2(f_1(C_2))) \cup \ldots$$

$$\bar{x}_2 = C_2 \cup f_2(f_1(C_2)) \cup f_2(f_1(f_2(f_1(C_2)))) \cup \ldots \qquad (3.6)$$

To achieve a numerical result, we can put for example:

$$f_1(x) = f_2(x) = f_3(x) = \frac{x}{2}$$

$$c_3 = 2 \quad , \quad C_2 = \{1\}$$

Thus the sets of solutions of problems P_1 and P_2 are in this case

$$x_1 = \left\{ \frac{1}{2}, \frac{1}{8}, \frac{1}{32} \ldots \right\} = \left\{ 2^{-2i-1} ; i = 0, 1, \ldots \right\}$$

$$\qquad (3.7)$$

$$x_2 = \left\{ 1, \frac{1}{4}, \frac{1}{16} \ldots \right\} = \left\{ 2^{-2i} ; i = 0, 1, \ldots \right\}$$

From the symbolic result (3.6), we point out that any solution of a problem P_i can be obtained by traversing the graph from V_i to some terminal V_k and applying in the reverse order to the constant c_k the functions corresponding to the arcs traversed. This is not a special case. In fact we can state the following theorem.

Theorem 3.1

Given a reduction graph G, let a reduction chain A of a problem P_i be any path in G from V_i to some terminal node V_k, and let its cost σ (A) be obtained by applying in the reverse order to constant c_k the functions corresponding to the arcs of the path A. Then the set of solutions of a problem P_i consists of the costs of exactly all its reduction chains.

This theorem can be easily proved using algorithm ITER and a well-known property of the symbolic powers of graph adjacency matrices. However, for a complete proof, see [12].

4. PROBLEM REDUCTION AND DYNAMIC PROGRAMMING

Given a problem P_i and its (nonempty) set of solutions $\bar{x}_i$, we feel that the result of a minimization process on P_i could be better defined as the greatest lower bound (glb) of $\bar{x}_i$ rather than as the minimum of $\bar{x}_i$. In fact such a definition will allow to find in all cases some result (*) and, furthermore, the result will be the same obtained by taking the set closure of $\bar{x}_i$ first, and the minimum afterwards. In a sense, such a definition is a formal way of introducing infinite reduction chains: in the example of Fig. 3 the infinite chain obtained by looping forever has clearly a cost of 0, which is the glb of the solutions of both P_1 and P_2.

To insure glb always exists, we transform the set of real numbers R into a complete lattice L_R by adding to R a top element ($+\infty$) and a bottom element ($-\infty$). A function $h_p : 2^R \to L_R$ which extends glb is now defined as follows:

$$(4.1) \qquad h_p(x) = \begin{cases} \text{if } x = \phi \text{ then } + \infty \\ \text{if glb(x) exists, then glb(x)} \\ \text{else } - \infty \end{cases}$$

Function h_p can be extended to n-tulpes as follows:

$$L_2 = (L_R)^n$$

(*) Here $-\infty$ must be considered a result.

$$H_p : L_1 \to L_2 \;\; ; \;\; (H_p)_i (x) = h_p (x_i)$$

Now, given a problem P_i and its solution set $\bar{x}_i$ we call the value $\bar{y}_i = h_p(\bar{x}_i)$ the minimal limit solution (mls) of problem P_i. Note again that a mls need not be a solution.

Function H_p defined above has the nice property of preserving the inverse order, namely if $x' \leqslant x''$ then $H_p(x') \geqslant H_p(x'')$. As a consequence, by applying H_p to the approximations generated by algorithm ITER, which form an ascending chain in L_1.

$$x_0 \leqslant x_1 \leqslant x_2 \leqslant \ldots$$

a descending chain in L_2 is obtained:

$$H_p(x_0) \geqslant H_p(x_1) \geqslant H_p(x_2) \geqslant \ldots$$

Such values give a closer and closer approximation of the n-tulpe of mls's of our problems. Note also that since all approximated sets of solutions generated by ITER are finite, for every nonempty such set x_i we have

$$y_i = h_p(x_i) = glb(x_i) = \min(x_i)$$

For our example in Fig. 3 we have for instance

$$x_1^0 = \phi \qquad x_2^0 = \phi \qquad y_1^0 = +\infty \qquad y_2^0 = +\infty$$

$$x_1^1 = \phi \qquad x_2^1 = \{1\} \qquad y_1^1 = +\infty \qquad y_2^1 = 1$$

$$x_1^2 = \left\{\frac{1}{2}\right\} \qquad x_2^2 = \{1\} \qquad y_1^2 = \frac{1}{2} \qquad y_2^2 = 1$$

$$x_1^3 = \left\{\frac{1}{2}\right\} \qquad x_2^3 = \left\{1, \frac{1}{4}\right\} \qquad y_1^3 = \frac{1}{2} \qquad y_2^3 = \frac{1}{4}$$

In general, no better procedure for computing mls's can be found, than passing through the sets of solutions. In a special case, however, a direct approach is possible: when all functions in the alphabet F are monotone (*).

(*) If a function $f \in F$ is monotone from R to R, it can be easily extended to obtain a monotone function from ./.

In fact, we can state the following thorem (see [12] for a proof).

Theorem 4.1.

Let f be a monotone function from R to R (or from 2^R to 2^R, when images are considered) and let h_p be the function from 2^R to L_R defined in (4.1). These two functions commute, i.e. for every $x \in 2^R$ we have:

(4.2) $h_p(f(x)) = f(h_p(x))$

As a consequence of the inverse order preserving property of h_p and of theorem 4.1, we can apply our h_p function to both sides of equation (3.1) and simplify it as follows;

$$h_p(S_i) \leqslant h_p(f_k(S_j))$$
$$h_p(S_i) \leqslant f_k(h_p(S_j))$$

Thus, letting $y_i = h_p(S_i)$, we get

(4.4) $y_i \leqslant f_k(y_j)$

Finally, we can take the minimum (in L_2) of all equations of type (4.4) having the same left member. If we represent the minimum operation with the sum symbols "+" and "Σ", we get (**)

(4.5) $y_i \leqslant \sum_{j=1}^{n} f_{ij}(y_j) + c_i$

Here, as obvious, we have

$$c_i = h_p(C_i) = \sum_{r=n+1}^{n+t} f_{ir}(c_r) \qquad i = 1, \dots, n$$

In the example in Fig. 2, if we assume that our functions are monotone, we can

---

./. L_R to L_R. It suffices to let

(4.3) $f(\pm \infty) = \lim_{x \to \pm \infty} f(x)$

Note that being f monotone, the limit always exists.

(**) Such symbols will be used in the sequel only in this sense, unless otherwise stated.

write

$$y_1 \leqslant \qquad\qquad f_1(y_2) + f_4(y_3)$$

$$y_2 \leqslant f_2(y_1) + f_3(y_2) \qquad\qquad + c_2$$

$$y_3 \leqslant \qquad\qquad f_1(y_2) \qquad\qquad + c_3$$

where

$$c_2 = f_4(c_4) + f_5(c_5)$$

$$c_3 = f_2(c_5) + f_1(c_6)$$

From the reasoning above, it follows in the monotone case that if S_i ($i = 1,...,n$) is a solution of system (3.2) then $y_i = h_p(S_i)$ ($i = 1,...,n$) is a solution of system (4.5). Furthermore, it is possible to give the following theorem (see [12] for a proof).

Theorem 4.2

Let $\overline{S}_i$ ($i = 1,...,n$) be the minimal solution of system (3.2) and let $\overline{y}_i$ ($i = 1,...n$) be the maximal (*) solution of system (4.5). We have:

$$\overline{y}_i = h_p(\overline{S}_i) \qquad i = 1, ... , n$$

From this theorem it follows that in the monotonic case the set of minimal limit solutions can be obtained by simply solving system (4.5), instead of solving system (3.2) first and then applying the greatest lower bound operator h_p to the solution.

System (4.5), written with the equal sign (**)

$$y_i = \sum_{j=1}^{n} f_{ij}(y_j) + c_i \qquad\qquad\qquad (4.6)$$

is again the system of functional equations of dynamic programming [1,5]. For instance, functional equations for the example in Fig. 3 are as follows:

$$y_1 = \frac{y_2}{2}$$

(*) Knaster-Tarsky theorem can be symmetrically stated for maximal instead of minimal solutions.

(**) According to fixpoint theorem, (4.5) and (4.6) have the same maximal fixpoint.

$$y_2 = \min\left(1, \frac{y_1}{2}\right)$$

Of course, if functions f_{ij} are continuous in L_R (*), then also $\bar{y}_i$ can be obtained by algorithm ITER (**), which in this case can be rewritten as follows

Algorithm MIN

Step 1 Let $y_i^o = +\infty$ $(i = 1,...,n); k = 1$.

Step 2 Let $y_i^k = \sum_{j=1}^{n} f_{ij}(y_j^{k-1}) + c_i$ $(i = 1, ... , n)$

Step 3 If $y_i^k = y_i^{k-1}$ $(i = 1,...,n)$ then stop: $y_i^k = \bar{y}_i$ is the minimal limit solution we sought; else let $k = k + 1$ and go to step 2.

As usual, when algorithm MIN does not terminate, it gives however an infinite descending chain of approximations whose limit is the mls. Note that this happens exactly when the mls is not a solution. For instance, in the example in Fig. 3 is clear that

$$y_i = \lim_{k\to\infty} y_i^k = 0 \ , \quad i = 1,2$$

However, we can see from (3.7) that $y_i = 0$ is not a solution.

5. CONCLUSION

In this paper we have presented a variant of the formal approach to dynamic programming due to Karp and Held. Instead of founding dynamic programming on automata theory and then deriving the functional equations, we have presented it in terms of a problem reduction model, which, we feel, is very close to the concept of problem embedding introduced originally by Bellman. In this process, we have introduced two lattices, the lattice of sets of solutions L_1 and the

---

(*) If a function f is continuous from R to R, its extension given by formula (4.3) is continuous in lattice L_R.

(**) More precisely, $\bar{y}_i$ can be computed by the dual of algorithm ITER.

lattice of minimal limit solutions L_2 which are homomorphic through a greatest lower bound operator. The problem reduction model allows to express the sets of solutions in terms of the minimal fixpoint of a function from L_1 to L_1, and an effective iterative method for approximating such sets of solutions can be given. Here the role of monotonicity becomes apparent, since it allows to derive a parallel system of equations in L_2 whose fixpoint is the set of minimal limit solutions and which, in turn, can be solved with an iterative algorithm. Such equations are the functional equations of dynamic programming.

Even if the two approaches have points in common (for instance, every solution generated by the iterative algorithm corresponds to a finite problem reduction chain, and thus to a sequence of decisions in Karp's model) we think that a distinct advantage of our approach is to give always a meaning to the solution of functional equations, i.e. to be the greatest lower bound of our sets of solutions. In Karp's approach, instead, a meaning is given only when sets of solutions have minima. Furthermore, we obtain a general iterative algorithm for solving functional equations, which descends immediately from our lattice fixpoint approach.

REFERENCES

[1]   Bellman, R.E., Dynamic Programming, Princeton University Press, Princeton N.J., 1957

[2]   Denardo, E.V., Contraction Mapping in the Theory Underlying Dynamic Programming, SIAM Rev., 9, 1967, pp. 165-177.

[3]   Mitten, L.G., Composition Principles for Synthesis of Optimal Multistage Processes, Operations Res., 12, 1964, pp. 610-619.

[4]   Nemhauser, G.L., Introduction to Dynamic Programming, Wiley, New York, 1966.

[5]   Karp, R.M. and Held, M., Finite-State Processes and Dynamic Programming, SIAM J. Appl. Math., 15, 1967, pp. 693-718.

[6]   Salomaa, A., Theory of Automata, Pergamon, 1969.

[7]   Ibaraki, T., Representation Theorems for Equivalent Optimization Problems, Information and Control, 21, N. 5, 1972, pp. 397-435.

[8]   Ibaraki, T., Solvable Classes of Discrete Dynamic Programming , J.Math. Anal. Appl., 43, 1973, pp. 642-693.

[9]   Nilsson, N.J., Problem-Solving Methods in Artificial Intelligence, McGraw--Hill, 1971.

[10]   Birkhoff, G., Lattice Theory, Am.Math.Soc., 1967.

[11]   Tarsky, A., A Lattice-Theoretical Fixpoint Theorem and its Applications, Pacific J. of Maths, 5, pp. 285-309.

[12]   Martelli, A. and Montanari, U., Problem Solving as a Foundation for Dynamic Programming, in preparation.

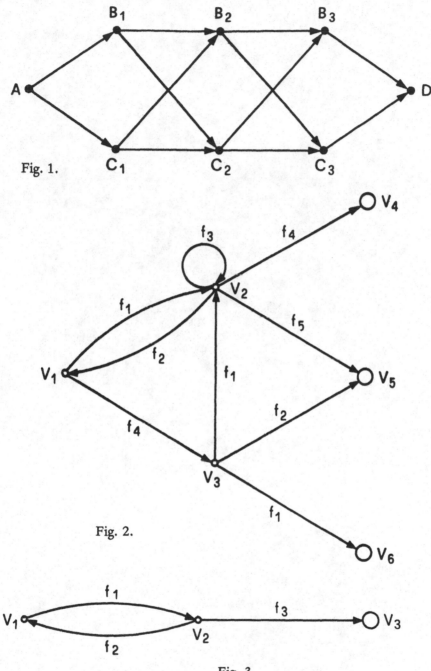

Fig. 1.

Fig. 2.

Fig. 3.

PARKING FUNCTIONS AND INFORMATION STRUCTURES (*)

F. LUCCIO (**)

1. INTRODUCTION

Data may take different forms, depending on the problem to which they pertain, and on the technique used to solve the problem. Such forms are referred to as **information structures**.

When a computer oriented approach is followed, information structures must be mapped onto memory structures. That is, data must be allocated in proper constructions of cells of a computer memory, such that all the characteristics of data are maintained, and all the operations required on data can be readily performed. We will discuss mapping of the most widely used information structure (the file) onto the simplest memeory structure (the vector).

A file F of size n is a set of n elements, each of which includes a name. The basic operation to be performed on F is the search for an element given the name. For any element, a search length S can be defiend as the number of elements encountered in the search. Efficiency of a search policy is then measured by the **average search length** $\bar{S}$, that is the average value of S for all the elements.

Possibly F is a dynamic structure, that is insertion and deletion of elements may be required on F during its use.

A **vector** V of size m is a set of m successive memory locations. Since we refer to a main computer memory, each location in V is accessed in a unit of time, once its address is specified. This feature is referred to as random access to V.

A file F of size n is mapped onto a vector V of size m (n ⩽ m) by allocating any element of F into a proper location of V. The allocation policy is the central subject of this work. (**) Two techniques are commonly used to map files

(*) The present study was carried out in cooperation with the Istituto di Elaborazione dell'Informazione del C.N. R., Pisa, Italy.

(**) Università di Pisa, Pisa, Italy.

(***) If there are elements in F requiring d memory locations to be stored (d > 1), V is ideally divided into s sections of d locations each, and each element of F is allocated in any such section (s · d = m, n ⩽ s). The ./ .

onto vectors. If no modification of the file is required during its use, then its elements can be stored according to some ordering of the names (e.g. alphabetic order), and a binary search on such names can be performed. As is well known this method is optimal for memory requirement (all the locations of V are actually used: m = n), but the average search length $\bar{S}$ is of the order of $\log_2$ n. (for details see [1]).

If the file is to be modified during its use by insertion or deletion of elements, then one of a family of mehtods is employed; these methods are grouped under the general name of "hash coding methods". The search for an element proceeds in V through a sequence of addresses. The first address is computed as a function of the name of the element. The subsequent addresses are evaluated by addition of a proper increment to the previous address in the sequence. Insertion of a new element is performed by a search for it, until an empty location is found; the element is then entered in such a location, and any subsequent search retrieves it there. (*) Deletion of elements is slightly more complex, however, this operation is less frequently required in general.

Search efficiency of hash coding methods can be substantially increased over the one of binary search, if V is not filled entirely. In fact, for all the hash coding methods practically in use, it can be generally stated that the average search length $\bar{S}$ is merely a (increasing) function of the ratio α = n/m, and that $\bar{S}$ maintains very low values for $\alpha \leqslant 0.9$, while it increases very rapidly for α approaching to 1. $\bar{S}$ is then independent of the size of F, if a fixed percent of computer memory is left unused. (For details see [2]).

The purpose of the present work is to discuss how, along the lines of hash coding, a special class of functions can be used as a mathematical basis to treat file allocation and searching. These functions are termed parking functions here, by extension of a classical definition.

The class of two level parking functions is also introduced, to treat files residing in a two level computer store.

./. use of sections of constant size still allows random access to (the sections of) V, and the whole matter contained in this study can be straightforwardly adapted to such a new situation.

(*) F is initially mapped onto V, by repeating the insertion process for any single element of the initial configuration of F.

2. PARKING PROBLEMS AND PARKING FUNCTIONS

Parking problems can be generally posed as follows. A parking area $[m] = \{0, 1, ..., m-1\}$ is given, into which n consecutive parkers from among the ones of a set $[p] = \{0, 1, ..., p-1\}$ search for a location. The relations hold:

$$p \geqslant m \quad ; \quad n \leqslant m. \tag{1}$$

A parking map h assigns a parking policy to any element of $[p]$:

$$h : [p] \times [k] \rightarrow [m] \tag{2}$$

where $[k] = \{0, 1, ... \}$ is the set of natural numbers.

In fact, h(i,j) specifies, for consecutive values of $j \epsilon [k]$, the search sequence to be traced by parker $i \epsilon [p]$ through the parking area, until an empty location is encountered, That is, i parks in the empty location h(i,j) (if any), with the minimum vlaue of j.

If all the n parkers find a place in $[m]$, independently of their selection from among the elements of $[p]$, and of their order of appearence, h is termed a **parking function**. (It is worthwhile to note that the original definition of parking functions, given by Konheim and Weiss in $[3]$ as a map $[m] \rightarrow [m]$, is a particualr subcase of the one given here. We have extended the definition to a form that will exhibit a relevance in the problem of file allocation and searching).

As an introductory example consider the following, which is possibly the simplest parking function of some interest:

$$h(i,j) = [i + j]_{mod\ m} \tag{3}$$

That is, the initial location $h(i,0) = [i]_{mod\ m}$ assigned to parker i is the reminder of the division between parker's name and size of parking area. If such a location is already occupied by another parker, i proceeds to the next locations $h(i,1) = [h(i,0) + 1]_{mod\ m}$, ..., $h(i,j) = [h(i,j-1) + 1]_{mod\ m}$, until an empty space is found. The addition of increment 1 is performed modulo m, that corresponds to have a cylcic parking area, where locations m-1 and 0 are contiguous.

Since the number of actual parkers does not exceed the number of available parking locations (see relations (1)), and the function (3) allows to search through all the parking locations, then every parker will certainly find a place in the parking area. That is, (3) is a parking function.

The whole situation is shown in fig. 1. We assume that the parking area can be accessed in any point: then, parker i tests location $[i]_{\bmod m}$ first, and, if such a location is taken, proceeds in the one-way driveway seeking for an empty place.

From the above presentation of parking functions it should be clear how they may constitute a mathematical description of file allocation and searching. In this perspective, $[p]$ is interpreted as the set of all possible names of file elements, (*) from which the n names of the elements in the file actually considered are selected; $[m]$ is interpreted as the set of vector locations; the sequence of locations specified by the function, for any file element, is traced for both initial allocation and subsequent retrival of the element. A general theory of parking functions does not exist thus far, however, most of the known hash coding methods can be formulated in terms of parking functions, and their properties interpreted in this new light.

When dealing with files, the major goal of any search method is the minimization of the average search length $\bar{S}$. That is, the optimal parking function must accomodate all parkers in a minimal average number of steps. It is to be noted, however, that the real figure to minimize should be the amount of total computation required by the search. Since the number and cost of the arithmetic operations to be performed for any step depends in general on the computer being used, then lowering the computation complexity is seen as an independent secondary goal. Heuristically we say that parking functions should exhibit a form leading to simple calculations (this point will be precisely characterized in section 4).

In order to have low values of $\bar{S}$, the starting strategy is to generate an even distribution of initial accesses over the parking area, for all the perspective parkers in $[p]$. This is substantiated by two concurrent facts, namely:

(i) the selection of n actual parkers from among the ones of $[p]$ depends on the particular file to be allocated;

(ii) it is assumed that all the possible selections in (i) have the same probability to occur.

If $p \gg m$, as is verified in common applications, then the initial access to $[m]$ is computed by the law:

(4) $h(i,0) = [i]_{\bmod m}$

(*) In a computer representation the names of elements are strings of bits, which may be directly interpreted as integers in a proper code.

which exhibits a fairly even distribution over [m], and requires very simple calculations.

　　　　We will now discuss a group of parking functions, in which the sequence of search locations is obtained by addition of a variable quantity q to the initial access. Namely:

$$h(i,j) = [i + q(i,j)]_{\bmod m} \qquad (5)$$

where:

$$q(i,0) = 0. \qquad$$

Note that q may be independent of i, however, it must always be a function of j.

　　　　The simplest form for (5) is linear in j, with a constant increment step:

$$h(i,j) = [i + a \cdot j]_{\bmod m} \qquad (6)$$

where:

　　　　a is an integer constant;
　　　　a is coprime with m.

It can be easily shown that relation (6) is a parking function if and only if a and m are coprime. (*)

　　　　As far as the average search length is concerned, parking function (6) describes the least efficient search policy in use; in fact, the search is affected by a serious **clustering** phenomenon. If

$$h(i_1, j_1) = h(i_2, j_2) \ , \quad i_1 \neq i_2 \ , \quad j_1 \neq j_2 \ ,$$

then

$$h(i_1, j_1 + 1) = h(i_2, j_2 + 1)$$

and the search for i_1 and i_2 then proceeds through the same locations, even though $h(i_1,0) \neq h(i_2,0)$. More specifically, a cluster is a set of occupied locations of [m], lying 'a' positions apart from one another. The effect of a cluster is to force parkers entering the cluster in different locations to trace a partially common sequence; this partially nullifies the advantage of having an even distribution of initial accesses.

(*) Parking function (3) already introduced is a particular case of (6).

Clusters rapidly expand for values of $\alpha = n/m$ approaching to 1, hereby affecting the average search length; a typical figure for parking function (6) is: $\bar{S} = 5.50$ for $\alpha = 0.9$.

The effect of clusters can be eliminated by altering the equidistance of successive locations in the search sequence. Different solutions have been proposed for this purpose, all putting some restrictions on the vector size m.

A quadratic form may be substituted for q in relation (5), giving rise to the function:

(7) $$h(i,j) = [i + a \cdot j + b \cdot j^2]_{\text{mod } m}$$

where:

a, b are integer constants; (*)
m is a prime number;
$n \leqslant (m + 1)/2$.

By applying relation (7) to any value of i, it results: for any pair of distinct values j_1, j_2, $0 \leqslant j_1, j_2 \leqslant (m-1)/2$:

(8.a) $$h(i,j_1) \neq h(i,j_2) ;$$

for any value $j_1 \geqslant (m + 1)/2$, there exists a value j_2, $0 \leqslant j_2 \leqslant (m-1)/2$:

(8.b) $$h(i,j_1) = h(i,j_2).$$

That is, in the first $(m + 1)/2$ steps of the search sequence, any parker i encounters exactly $(m + 1)/2$ distinct locations. In the subsequent steps, i traces indefinitely through locations already encountered. The above assertions rely upon a known property of prime numbers; for a proof of their validity see [4].

Relations (8.a,b) indicate that (7) is a parking function if and only if $n \leqslant (m + 1)/2$; that is, one half of the vector space must be left unused.

To overcome the above limitation on n, a substantially more complex quadratic law has been suggested in [5]. In terms of parking functions, we can write:

(*) The simplest non trivial choice of values for a and b is: $a = 0, b = 1$.

$$h(i,j) = \left[2i + m - [i + j^2]_{\text{mod } m} \right]_{\text{mod } m'} \quad j \in \{0,2,4,\dots,m-1\};$$

$$(9.\text{a})$$

$$h(i,j) = [i + j^2]_{\text{mod } m'} \qquad\qquad\qquad j \in \{1,3,\dots,m\}; \qquad (9.\text{b})$$

where:

m is a prime number of the form m = 4g + 3, with positive integer g.

No limitation has been posed on n, in fact, relations (9.a,b) allow searching through all the locations in [m]. Therefore, (9.a,b) is a parking function. (Note that, for j = 0, relation (9.a) gives the correct value: $h(i,0) = [i]_{\text{mod } m}$).

In first approximation, parking functions (7) and (9.a) are not effected by clustering. Therefore, in the common range of α : $\alpha \leqslant 0.5$, such functions yield the same values of $\bar{S}$, which are substantially decreased over the ones of the linear search (6). A typical figure for parking function (9.a,b) is: $\bar{S} = 2.79$ for $\alpha = 0.9$.

Other sequences with variable increment have been proposed, for a vector containing m = 2^r locations. (The relevance of such vectors will be discussed in section 4). One sequence has the form:

$$h(i,j) = [i + p(j)]_{\text{mod } m} \qquad\qquad (10)$$

where:

m = 2^r;

p(j) is produced by a pseudorandom number generator.

One such generator has been given by Morris (see [2] for the algorithm, which involves a few programming steps).

Morris' generator produces all the integers in the interval 1 ÷ m-1, in an order such that $p(j_1 + 1) - p(j_1) \neq p(j_2 + 1) - p(j_2)$ for any couple $j_1 \neq j_2$. If Morris' generator is used, (10) is a parking function. The absence of clustering yields values of $\bar{S}$ which coincide with the ones observed for functions (7) and (9.a,b).

The sequence most recently proposed makes use of a linear form in j, whose increment step is a function of i [6]. Namely:

$$h(i,j) = [i + [2 \cdot [i]_{\text{mod } m} + 1]_{\text{mod } m} \cdot j]_{\text{mod } m} \qquad (11)$$

where
$$m = 2^r.$$

In order to prove that relation (11) is a parking function, we note that parker i proceeds in a linear search with increment step:

(12) $a(i) = [2 \cdot [i]_{mod\ m} + 1]_{mod\ m}$.

a(i) is an odd number for any value of i, that is, a(i) is coprime with m. As already pointed out in connection with form (6), such a condition proves that (11) is a parking function.

The absence of clustering still produces values of $\bar{S}$ coincident with the ones of parking functions (7), (9.a,b) and (10). However, relation (11) may be preferred to all others, since it involves surprisingly simple calculations. A discussion on this point will be given in section 4.

3. PARKING IN A TWO LEVEL AREA

Let us now assume that the parking area is composed of several blocks, and that passing from one block to another requires substantially more time than passing from one position to another within the same block.

The m parking locations are arranged into m_1 blocks of m_2 locations each, $m = m_1 \cdot m_2$. A parking map is defined as:

(13) $h : [p] \times [k] \rightarrow [m_1] \times [m_2]$

where:

$[m_1] = \{0, 1, ..., m_1 - 1\}$ is the set of blocks;
$[m_2] = \{0, 1, ..., m_2 - 1\}$ is the set of locations in each block;
the usual interpretation holds for [p] and [k].

$h(i,j) = h_1(i,j), h_2(i,j)$ specifies the search sequence to be traced by parker i at consecutive steps j, as a series of pairs of integers which indicate the block to be accessed ($h_1(i,j)$) and the in-block location ($h_2(i,j)$). If all parkers in a group of n (n $\leq$ m) find a location in $[m_1] \times [m_2]$, independently of their selection from [p] and of their order of appeerance, h is termed a two level parking function.

Under the timing assumption already posed, we can heuristically assert that the search sequence must remain in the same block as far as possible, before accessing a new block.

Possibly, the simplest two level parking function of some interest is given by:

$$h_1(i,j) = [\lfloor (i+j)/m_2 \rfloor]_{\bmod m_1} \qquad (14.a)$$

$$h_2(i,j) = [i+j]_{\bmod m_2} \qquad (14.b)$$

where:

$\lfloor x \rfloor$ indicates the integral part of x.

The initial location for parker i is:

$$h_1(i,0) = [\lfloor i/m_2 \rfloor]_{\bmod m_1} \qquad (15.a)$$

$$h_2(i,0) = [i]_{\bmod m_2} \qquad (15.b)$$

that is, block $h_1(i,0)$ is specified by the quotient of the division between parker's name and block size – modulo the number of blocks; the in-block location $h_2(i,0)$ is specified by the reminder of the above division. If location $h(i,0)$ is occupied, parker i proceeds through the locations (for $j \geqslant 1$):

$$h_2(i,j) = [h_2(i,j-1) + 1]_{\bmod m_2},$$

$$\text{if} \quad h_2(i,j) = 0 \text{ then}$$

$$h_1(i,j) = [h_1(i,j-1) + 1]_{\bmod m_1}$$

$$\text{else}$$

$$h_1(i,j) = h_1(i,j-1),$$

until an empty place is found. That is, i traces through adjacent locations up to the end of the block, then proceeds from the first location of next block. Since blocks m_1-1 and 0 are adjacent, the parking area is cyclic. The whole situation is shown in

fig. 2.

Relations (14a,b) allow searching through all the m locations of the parking area, hence, such relations constitute a two level parking function.

Two level parking functions may constitute a mathematical description of file allocation and searching in a paged environment. That is, the parking area $[m_1] \times [m_2]$ is interpreted as a set of m_1 vectors (pages) of size m_2 each, such that moving through the current vector is less costly than accessing a new vector. Therefore, if the sequence does not generally affect more than one block, a major goal of searching in two levels still is the minimization of the average search length $\bar{S}(\alpha)$, $\alpha = n/m$. (The relevance of paged memory structures, and the relative timing figures, will be discussed in the next section).

As usual, the starting strategy in designing a two level parking function is to produce an even distribution of initial accesses over the parking area, for all the perspective parkers in $[\,p\,]$. This is simply achieved by relations (15.a,b). (*)

The subsequent search steps may be obtained by addition of two variable quantities q_1 and q_2 to the initial accesses to $[m_1]$ and $[m_2]$, respectively:

$$(16.a) \qquad h_1(i,j) = [h_1(i,0) + q_1(i,j)]_{\mod m_1}$$

$$(16.b) \qquad h_2(i,j) = [h_2(i,0) + q_2(i,j)]_{\mod m_2}$$

where:

$$q_1(i,0) = q_2(i,0) = 0.$$

In the simplest form, q_1 and q_2 depend only on j; (16.a) is a step function; (16.b) is a linear function. Namely:

$$(17.a) \qquad h_1(i,j) = [\lfloor i/m_2 \rfloor + a_1 \cdot \lfloor j/m_2 \rfloor]_{\mod m_1}$$

$$(17.b) \qquad h_2(i,j) = [i + a_2 \cdot j]_{\mod m_2}$$

(*) Relations (15.a,b) generate an even distribution over $[m_1] \times [m_2]$, under the common hypothesis $p \gg m$.

The relations could instead be used:

$$h_1(i,0) = [i]_{\mod m_1}, \quad h_2(i,0) = [i]_{\mod m_2}.$$

under the less restrictive conditions $p \gg m_1$, $p \gg m_2$.

where:

a$_1$ and a$_2$ are integer constants;

a$_1$ is coprime with m$_1$, a$_2$ is coprime with m$_2$.

For $0 \leqslant j \leqslant$ m-1 all the locations in $[m_1] \times [m_2]$ are searched for, hence, relations (17.a,b) constitute a two level parking function. Furthermore, all the locations in any block are visited before a new block is accessed. (*) Search (17.a,b) is obviously affected by clustering at both levels, hence, the values of the average length $\bar{S}$ practically coincide with the ones for the linear search in one level (see section 2).

Clustering can be eliminated in a two level search, if cluster-free sequences are used for h$_1$ and h$_2$. However, if the search sequence does not exceed a single block for most parkers, the real improvement on the average search length is obtained by elimination of clustering from h$_2$. In this perspective, the most relevant two level search is given by a step function in j for h$_1$ (see (17.a)), and a linear function in j, whose increment step is a function of i, for h$_2$ (see (11)). Namely:

$$h_1(i,j) = [\lfloor i/m_2 \rfloor + \lfloor j/m_2 \rfloor]_{\text{mod } m_1} \qquad (18.a)$$

$$h_2(i,j) = [i + [2 \cdot [i]_{\text{mod } m_2} + 1]_{\text{mod } m_2} \cdot j]_{\text{mod } m_2} \qquad (18.b)$$

where:

$$m_2 = 2^{r_2}.$$

From previous discussions it follows that relations (18.a,b) constitute a two level parking function, such that in-block search is completed before a new block is accessed.

The values of $\bar{S}$ for the present search practically coincide with the values for quadratic search in one level (see section 2); in addition, relations (18.a,b) involve simple calculations. A discussion on this point is given in the next section.

(*) The simplest non trivial values for a$_1$ and a$_2$ are: a$_1$ = a$_2$ = 1. Note that the two level parking function (14.a,b) already introduced is not a particular case of (17.a,b).

4. TIMING CONSIDERATIONS

The present study is oriented towards computer applications of parking functions. In this light, evaluation of complexity of any function must take into account some peculiar aspects of computer processing.

Privileged vectors are the ones of size $m = 2^r$. In fact, relative addressing in such vectors is given by the set of all r-bit binary numbers (integers from 0 to $2^r - 1$), and the operation $[x]_{mod\ m}$ is simply performed by retaining the r least significant bits of x. The cost of the above operation is one machine instruction (masking) in most computers, while a division is generally required for $m \neq 2^r$.

When dealing with file processing, the average search length is in first approximation the most significant parameter to characterize the efficiency of a searching technique. However, the exact figure to be minimized is the average access time T to an element. For one level memory, T can be expressed by:

(19) $$T = t_a + (\bar{S}(\alpha) - 1) \cdot t_s + \bar{S}(\alpha) \cdot t_c$$

where:

t_a is the initial access time (for computing the initial access location);

t_s is the searching time for any subsequent step (for computing a new location in the sequence);

t_c is the time for name comparison (element retrieval) or for testing an empty location (element allocation).

The values of T depend on vector size, parking functions and computer being used. The following considerations are in order.

1. Under relation (4), the initial access time t_a is minimum for $m = 2^r$ (see the above discussion on the operation $[x]_{mod\ m}$); such a vector size is compatible with parking functions (6), (10) and (11).

2. The searching time t_s is minimum for the linear forms ((6) and (11)), sicne any address in the sequence can be evaluated by addition of an increment to the previous address. Function (6) makes use of a fixed increment; function (11) makes use of the variable increment (12), however, its value is computed once for any element i by extremely simple calculations ($[i]_{mod\ m}$ is known as initial access for i; multiplication by 2 and addition of 1 modulo $m = 2^r$ require a few machine instructions in any computer). Since the addition of increment is

performed modulo m, vectors of size $m = 2^r$ are still privileged.

3. The time for name comparison, t_c, is obviously independent of the parking function.

4. For the average search length $\bar{S}(\alpha)$ see section 2.

From an overall evaluation of all the parking functions previously discussed, relation (11) seems to emerge in general as the most efficient searching technique.

When the search is performed in two levels, the above timing considerations must be modified. In fact, the file is subdivided into blocks, and block access time is also to be considered. This is the case of a file residing in secondary storage, and transferred in pages into core memory; block access time is typically the time to load a new page. (*) A second case is the one of a file residing in core memory of a minicomputer with a paged organization, where addressing is performed via an index register containing the base address of a page. Block access time is then the time to reload the index register. In any case, page size typically is a power of two: $m_2 = 2^{r_2}$.

In the present case, the average access time T to an element can be expressed by:

$$T = t_a + (\bar{S}(\alpha) - 1) \cdot t_s + \bar{S}(\alpha) \cdot t_c + b \cdot t_b$$

where:

t_a, t_s and t_c have the same meaning as in (19) (t_a and t_s refer to the computation of block number and in-block location);

b   is the average number of blocks accessed in the sequence;

t_b is the block access time.

The following considerations are now in order.

1. Under the usual assumptions: $m_1 \leqslant 2^{r_1}$ (where r_1 is the smallest integer verifying the condition); $m_2 = 2^{r_2}$; $m \leqslant 2^r$ ($r = r_1 + r_2$); and under the

---

(*) In time shared computers the file is loaded in the memory of a virtual machine, but, in fact, resides in secondary storage and is transferred in pages into the physical memory. If a "logical page" in the virtual memory is exactly allocated in a "physical page" in core memory (see for example the IBM CP-67), then a file can be conducted to start at the beginning of a page, and a two level searching sequence can be directly programmed by the user.

relations (15.a,b); the initial access time t_a essentially is the time to perform one division. In fact, $h_2(i,0)$ and $h_1(i,0)$ can be respectively evaluated as the r_2 least significant bits, and the r_1 next bits, of the remainder of the division between i and m (if $m = 2^r$, such a division reduces to a masking operation),

2. The searching time t_s is substantially affected by the computation of the block number (relations (17.a) and (18.a)). In fact, both divisions required in such a computation (evaluation of $\lfloor j/m_2 \rfloor$, and addition modulo m_1) can be simply substituted by tests and subtractions, due to the constant increment of j. For the evaluation of in-block locations (17.b) and (18.b) see the previous discussions for (6) and (11).

3. Times t_c and t_b are independent of the parking function.

4. For parking funcions (17.a,b) and (18.a,b), a precise evaluation of the average number of accessed blocks b is quite intrigued. However, an upper bound to such a figure is given by the value relative to the function (14.a,b), which can be easily computed as:

(21) $$b = (\bar{S}(\alpha) - 1)/m_2$$

where $\bar{S}(\alpha)$ is the average search length for the linear search in one level. Relation (21) shows that the values of b are practically maintained very low, even in the worst cases (high value of α, small block size); for $\alpha = 0.9$ ($\bar{S}(\alpha) = 5.50$) and $m_2 = 128$, it results: $b = 0.035$.

5. Because of the low values of b (point 4.), the values of $\bar{S}(\alpha)$ for functions (17.a,b) and (18.a,b) practically coincide with the ones for linear and quadratic search in one level, respectively.

From the above considerations, function (18.a,b) appears as a very efficient technique for searching in two levels.

REFERENCES

[1] F.R.A. Hopgood, Compiling Techniques. American Elsevier Publ. Co. New York 1957. Ch. 4.

[2] R. Morris, Scatter storage techniques. Communications of the ACM, 11,1 (Jan. 1968), 38 − 43.

[3] A.S. Konheim and B. Weiss, An occupancy discipline and applications. SIAM J. Applied Mathematics, 14 (1966), 1266 − 1274.

[4] W.D. Maurer, An improved hash code for scatter storage. Communications of the ACM, 11,1 (Jan. 1968), 35-38.

[5] C.E. Radke, The use of quadratic residue research. Communications of the ACM, 13,2 (Feb. 1970), 103 − 105.

[6] F. Luccio, Weighted increment linear search for scatter tables. Communications of the ACM, 15,12 (Dec. 1972), 1045 − 1047.

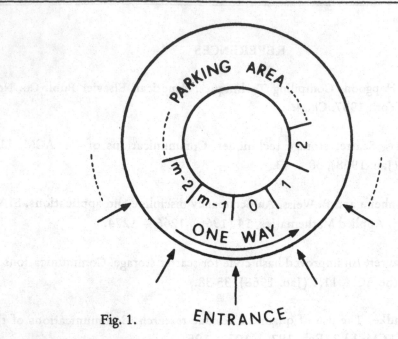

Fig. 1.

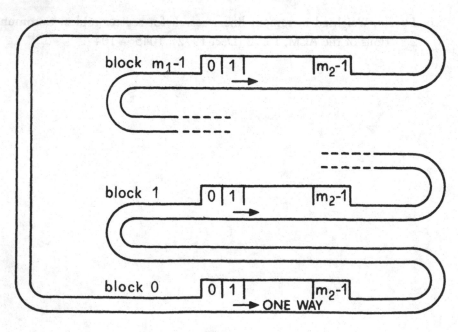

Fig. 2.

AN INTRODUCTION TO MATROID OPTIMIZATION (*)

E.L. Lawler (**)

1. INTRODUCTION

The theory of matroids has provided a significant extension of network flow theory and has greatly enlarged the class of problems which can be solved in a polynomial-bounded number of computational steps. We provide a very brief sketch of matroid optimization techniques, and refer the reader to the forthcoming book of the author for more elaboration.

2. MATROID DEFINITIONS

Matroid theory was founded by Hassler Whitney in 1935 as a product of his investigations of the algebraic theory of linear independence.

Consider a matrix whose elements are from an arbitrary field. Any subset of the columns of the matrix is either linearly independent or linearly dependent. The family of linearly independent sets is not at all arbitrary. For example, any subset of a linearly independent set is also linearly independent. Also, if I_p and I_{p+1} are independent sets of p and p + 1 columns respectively, then I_p together with some column of I_{p+1} forms an independent set of p + 1 columns.

On the other hand, there are algebraic systems that satisfy the above two properties but do not correspond to subsets of columns of any matrix. Algebraic systems which thus generalize these properties of matrices are known as "matroids".

Definition

A matroid $M = (E, \vartheta)$ is a structure in which E is a finite set of elements and ϑ is a family of subsets of E, such that

(*) This work has been supported by the Air Force Office of Scientific Research Grant 71-2076.

(**) Dept. of Electrical Engineering and Computer Science, University of California at Berkeley, U.S.A.

(2.1) $\phi \in \vartheta$ and all proper subsets of a set I in ϑ are in ϑ.

(2.2) If I_p and I_{p+1} are sets in ϑ containing p and p + 1 elements respectively, then there exists an element $e \in I_{p+1} - I_p$ such that

$$I_p \cup \{e\} \in \vartheta .$$

Much of the terminology of matroid theory is drawn from linear algebra and other terminology from graph theory. For example, a subset I in ϑ is said to be an independent set of the matroid M = (E, ϑ). A maximal independent set is said to be a base of the matroid, and the rank r(A) of a subset $A \subseteq E$ is the cardinality of a maximal independent set in A. (All maximal independent sets must have the same cardinality). A minimal dependent set is a circuit. The span of a set $A \subseteq E$, denoted sp(A), is the (unique) maximal superset of A in E having the same rank as A. Clearly, if B is a base, then sp(B) = E, i.e., "a base spans the matroid". A set A which is its own span is said to be a closed set.

Let us consider some examples of matorids:

Matric Matroids — Any matroid whose family of independent sets is isomorphic to the family of linearly independent sets of columns of a matrix is said to be the matroid of the matrix. Such a matroid is matric.

Graphic Matroids — Let G = (N,A) be a graph. Then the graphic matroid of that graph has as its elements the arcs of the graph and as its independent sets the subsets of arcs which do not contain cycles; such subsets form trees or forests of trees in the graph. The cographic matroid has as its independent sets the subsets of arcs which do not contain cocycles.

Transversal Matroids — Let G = (S,T,A) be a bipartite graph whose nodes are partitioned into sets S and T (each arc extending between these parts). A subset $I \subseteq S$ is said to be assignable if there exists a matching in the graph covering all the nodes in I. A transversal matroid is formed by taking S as the set of elements and the family of assignable subsets of S as its independent sets.

Partition Matroids — Let E be a finite set of elements and π be an arbitrary partition of E into disjoint blocks. A partition matroid is formed by taking as its independent sets all subsets of E which do not contain more than one element from any block of the partition.

All of the matroids mentioned above happen to be matiric matroids, although, as we have mentioned, there are non-matric matroids. The reader can see, for example, that the graphic matroid of a graph G is the matric matroid of the node-arc incidence of G, with arithmetic in the field of two elements. The reader should also be able to see that every partition matroid is a transversal matroid.

One of the more interesting aspects of matroid theory is that every matroid has a dual. If $M = (E, \vartheta)$ is a matroid, then its dual $M^D = (E, \vartheta^D)$ is such that $I^D \in \vartheta^D$ if and only if $E - I^D$ contains a base of M. The dual of a graphic matroid of a graph is the cographic matroid of the same graph. This duality relation holds whether or not the graph itself has a (graphic) dual.

3. THE GREEDY ALGORITHM

Suppose the elements of a matroid $M = (E, \vartheta)$ are assigned numerical weights. The first optimization problem we shall consider is that of finding an independent set $I \in \vartheta$ such that the sum of the weights of the elements in I is maximal.

This optimization problem can be solved by means of the so-called greedy algorithm, as follows. Build up the optimal independent set as follows. First, choose the element with the largest weight, then the element with the second largest, etc., (breaking ties arbitrarily), rejecting an element only if its weight is negative or if its introduction into the solution destroys independence. (The algorithm is called "greedy" because at each step the choicest possible morsel is chosen.)

Note that the efficiency of the greedy algorithm depends upon the efficiency with which it is possible to test for the independence of an arbitrary subset of elements. If a polynomial bounded subroutine is available for this purpose, then the overall algorithm is polynomial-bounded.

An example of the matroid greedy algorithms is Kruskal's procedure for finding a maximal spanning tree in an arc-weighted graph. In that case, the desired spanning tree is a maximal weight independent set of the graphic matroid of the graph.

Most significantly, not only does the greedy algorithm work for all matroids, it works only for matroids in a technical sense that we shall not make precise here.

4. MATROID INTERSECTIONS

Suppose $M_1 = (E, \vartheta_1)$ and $M_2 = (E, \vartheta_2)$ are two given matroids over the same set of numerically weighted elements E. We may now seek to find a maximum-weight set I that is independent in each of the two matroids, i.e., $I \in \vartheta_1 \cap \vartheta_2$.

The bipartite matching (assignment) problem represents a special case of the matroid intersection problem in which both M_1 and M_2 are partition matroids induced by the incidence relations of the arcs on the nodes of the graph. Thus, the matroid intersection problem generalizes the bipartite matching problem. And since network flow problems can be reduced to bipartite matching problems, matroid intersection theory generalizes network flow theory.

It is perhaps not surprising that algorithms for solving the matroid intersection problem parallel and generalize the classic matching algorithms. That is, the computation proceeds through successive augmentations of feasible solutions, with "augmenting sequences" replacing "augmenting paths." For this, the reader is referred to the author's forthcoming book.

There is a duality theory for matroid intersections which generalizes the duality theory of bipartite matching (König-Egervary Theorem) and network flows (Max-Flow Min-Cut Theorem). We state the following theorem without proof. We say that a pair of subsets E_1, E_2 of E is a covering of E if $E_1 \cup E_2 = E$. With respect to a given pair of matroids M_1, M_2, we define the rank of a covering $\& = (E_1, E_2)$ to be $r(\&) = r^1(E_1) + r^2(E_2)$, where r^1, r^2 denote ranks in M_1, M_2 respectively.

Matroid Intersection Duality Theorem

For any two matroids $M_1 = (E, \vartheta_1)$, $M_2 = (E, \vartheta_2)$ the maximum cardinality of a set $I \in \vartheta_1 \cap \vartheta_2$ is equal to the maximum rank of a covering $\& = (E_1, E_2)$.

5. MATROID MATCHING AND MATROID PARITY PROBLEMS

We now define a class of problems which simultaneously generalizes both the matroid intersection problem and the graphical nonbipartite matching problem. We shall give two alternative formulations which, by appropriate problem reductions, can be shown to be equivalent.

Matroid Matching Problem

Let $G = (N, A)$ be an arc-weighted graph and $M = (N, \vartheta)$ be a matroid with the nodes of G as its elements. We seek a maximum-weight matching in G, subject to the constraint that the nodes covered by the matching are an independent set of M.

Matroid Parity Problem

Let $M = (E, \vartheta)$ be a matroid whose elements are numerically weighted and arranged in pairs. That is, for each element e ∈ E, there is a uniquely defined mate ē. We seek to find a maximum weight independent set I of M, subject to the constraint that e ∈ I if and only if ē ∈ I.

It is believed that polynomial bounded algorithms may exist for these problems. But unfortunately, the discovery of these algorithms has remained just beyond our grasp.

6. (APPARENTLY) NONPOLYNOMIAL-BOUNDED GENERALIZATIONS

It would be gratifying to be able to solve certain generalizations of the problems defined above. For example, it would be particularly useful to be able to efficiently compute an optimal intersection of three matroids, rather than just two. Then we should be able to solve the traveling salesman problem, which can be shown to be equivalent to a problem involving the intersection of three matroids: two partition matroids and a graphic matroid.

There is no known polynomial-bounded computation for the intersection of three matroids. The author has shown that there exists a polynomial-bounded computation for the intersection of three matroids if and only if there exists a polynomial bounded computation for the intersection of k matorids, for any k ⩾ 3.

The author believes it likely that the matroid matching problem in some sense represents an extreme point of the class of problems which can be solved in polynomial time. However, it will certainly require much more research to prove this assertion in some precise form.

REFERENCES

[1]   J. Edmonds, "Matroids and the Greedy Algorithm", Math Progr., 1 (1971), 127 - 136.

[2]   D. Gale, "Optimal Assignments in an Ordered Set: An Application of Matroid Theory", J. Comb. Theory, 4 (1968) 176- 180.

[3]   J.B. Kruskal, "On the Shortest Spanning Tree of a Graph and the Traveling Salesman Problem", Proc. Amer. Math.Soc., 7 (1956), 48-50.

[4]   E.L. Lawler, Combinatorial Optimization, Chapters 7 - 9, to be published by Holt, Rinehart and Winston.

Printed in the United States
By Bookmasters